the BIG title

NBA 2000 CHAMPION LOS ANGELES LAKERS

BY BARRY RUBINSTEIN & LYLE SPENCER

PHOTOGRAPHY BY NBA ENTERTAINMENT PHOTOS

DESIGNED AND PRODUCED BY RARE AIR MEDIA

CREDITS

Text by: Barry Rubinstein and Lyle Spencer. Rubinstein joined NBA Editorial in 1999. Previously, he was a writer and editor for 20 years for the *Newark Star-Ledger* and the *Morristown Daily Record*. Spencer is a sports columnist for the *Riverside Press-Enterprise*. He has been a writer for 30 years, also covering sports for the *New York Post*, *National Sports Daily* and *Santa Monica Evening Outlook*.

Designed and Produced by: Rare Air Media
1711 N. Paulina, Suite 311, Chicago, IL 60622

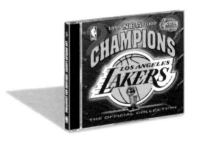

SPECIAL THANKS

From Barry Rubinstein:
To my wife Karen: Thanks for your inspiration and your love

From Lyle Spencer:
To my very special daughters Kimberly and Rachael

At NBA Editorial
Jan Hubbard, Jeanne Tang, John Hareas, Chris Ekstrand, John Gardella, Tracey Reavis,
Rob Reheuser, Rita Sullivan, April Bulger, Phillip Mirrer-Singer

At NBA Photos:
Carmin Romanelli, Joe Amati, Jesse Garrabrant, David Bonilla, Pam Healy, Michael Klein
Scott Yurdin, John Kristofick, Bennett Renda, Chris Chambers

At the NBA:
David Stern, Russ Granik, Brian McIntyre, Terry Lyons

At NBA Entertainment:
Adam Silver, Gregg Winik, Heidi Ueberroth, Charles Rosenzweig, Paul Hirschheimer,
Marc Hirschheimer, Michael Levine, Meredith Tanchum

At Rare Air Media:
Mark Vancil, Jim Forni, John Vieceli, Andy Pipitone, Mark Alper, Shereen Boury,
Dennis Carlson, Melinda Fry, Seth Guge, Elizabeth Fulton, Steve Polacek

At Doubleday Broadway:
Michael Palgon, Peter Gethers

Also:
Phil Jackson, Jim Perzik, John Black, Tim Harris and the entire Lakers organization,
Larry Bird, Dale Raterman, David Benner and the entire Pacers organization

Andrew D. Bernstein	Pages – front cover, 9,10,11,13,14-15,16,17, 19,20,21,22,23,26,27,28,29,30, 31,32,33,35,36,38,39,40,41,42,43,44,48,49,	Andy Hayt	Pages – front cover,6,45,52,54,58,59,61,62, 75,85,91,93, back cover
	50,51,53,55,59,60,62,63,67,68, 70,71,73,75,77,78,79,80,81,83,84,85,86, 87,90,92,93,94,95, back cover	Ron Hoskins	Pages – 75,84,86
		Atiba Jefferson	Pages – 24-25,96
		Robert C. Mora	Page – 94
Nathaniel S. Butler	Pages – front cover, 20,52,53,54,56,57, 58,63,64,65,66,67,68,69,72,76,77,78,82,88, 89,90,92,94, back cover	Fernando Medina	Pages – 34,67,74
		Norm Perdue	Page – 36
		Wen Roberts	Page – 39
Gary Dineen	Page – 79	Scott Quintard	Pages – 8,12
Garrett Ellwood	Page – 37	Rocky Widner	Pages – 29,34
Jesse Garrabrant	Pages – 2-3,46-47,78		
Barry Gossage	Pages – 39,60-61		

CONTENTS

the CHAMPIONS

They craned their necks and contorted their bodies, stood on tiptoes and hung perilously from any appendage that would support their weight. They leaned from open office windows and traffic over-passes and dangled their legs from fire escapes and tree limbs. The more adventurous somehow managed to pull themselves atop standing traffic signals. All were intent on getting a better view, any view at all, of their conquering heroes.

Many of them had never seen anything like this before; a championship parade meandering its way down Figueroa Street in downtown Los Angeles. A vast number were too young to remember or hadn't even been born the last time their city was host to such an event.

They made noise, blared air horns, hooped and hollered. They pointed at the sight of a familiar face waving and beaming atop one of five open-air double-decker buses making their way slowly down the thoroughfare; a hulking 7-1, 315-pound man who was the biggest reason – literally as well as figuratively – for this gathering.

HARPER

> "We're going to get one next year, too."
>
> Shaquille O'Neal

SHAQ

KOBE

They saw another figure, a stylish, youthful, energizing force with a floppy hat atop his Afro.

And there was the salt-and-pepper-haired, bespectacled man, who was new to the celebration in this town, but no stranger to this kind of block party.

Shaq, Kobe and Phil. O'Neal, Bryant and Jackson. A trio for the millennium – at least in the opinion of an estimated crowd of 250,000 who gathered in downtown Los Angeles to celebrate the Lakers' NBA 2000 title.

It was evident that the good old days had returned because a long lost friend also showed up for the first time since 1988. Shiny, gold and gleaming, the Larry O'Brien Trophy returned to City of Angels for the seventh time since the Lakers left Minneapolis, where the franchise won an additional five titles in the 1950s.

So overpowering were the Lakers, particularly O'Neal, the NBA Finals Most Valuable Player, that the anticipation of future conquests was almost as exciting as the newly won title. Indeed, O'Neal captured the spirit of a past Lakers era when he mimicked former L.A. coach Pat Riley, who in the 1987 championship celebration guaranteed a repeat for the next season.

"We're going to get one next year, too," O'Neal told the crowd.

Who would argue? All season, the Lakers were widely regarded as a

Who would argue? All season, the Lakers were widely regarded as a juggernaut, the strongest team in the NBA. They finished the regular season 67-15.

juggernaut, the strongest team in the NBA. They finished the regular season 67-15, and although they were extended the distance in two of their four playoff series and taken to task for failing to exhibit a killer instinct at times, none of that mattered in the end.

Not to O'Neal, who became only the third player to win the scoring championship, the regular-season MVP and Finals MVP in the same year, joining Kareem Abdul-Jabbar and Michael Jordan. Not to Bryant, charming and wise beyond his 21 years, a player already being held up in comparison to the incomparable Jordan. And not to Jackson, the coach who saw in this team the possibility for all of this, and the pinnacle they never knew was possible until he came along with six NBA rings from Chicago.

The trio helped formulate a flashback to the "Showtime" era of the 1980s and the greatness of previous Lakers champions. Jerry West and Earvin "Magic" Johnson, Laker executives and visible links to that glorious past, can now confidently pass the torch to a new generation. O'Neal made that connection a number of times during the season, calling himself "The Big Continuous," to honor that legacy that stretched from him to Abdul-Jabbar, to Wilt Chamberlain and to George Mikan, who led the Lakers to those five titles in Minneapolis.

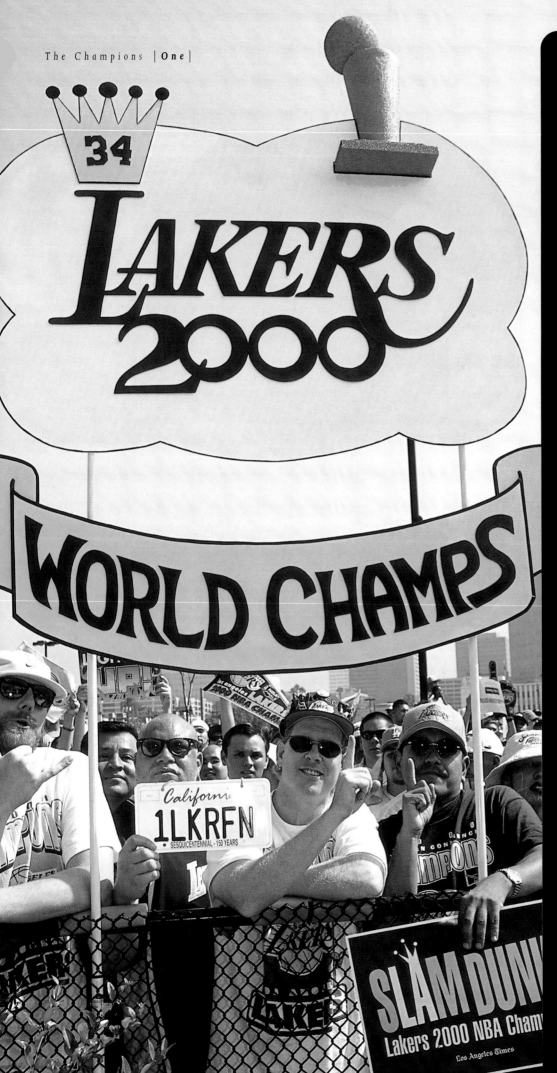

LAKERS 2000

WORLD CHAMPS

> "From now on, I am no longer 'The Big Aristotle.' I want to be known as 'The Big Shakespeare,' because it was Shakespeare who said, 'Some men are born great, some achieve greatness and some have greatness thrust upon them.'"
>
> Shaquille O'Neal

For Lakers owner Dr. Jerry Buss, it was a sixth championship. For West, the architect of the team who has been with Lakers for 38 of the past 40 years but won only one championship as a player, it was a seventh ring. For the rest of the team, it was proof of their value, even though it was evident that as O'Neal and Bryant went, so went the Lakers.

Still, Shaq and Kobe received considerable aid from the likes of Glen Rice, one of the league's top sharpshooters who sacrificed personal success — albeit, sometime reluctantly — in order to win a championship; Ron Harper, who brought three rings with him from Chicago and won his fourth; A.C. Green, the iron man of the NBA who has appeared in a record 1,110 consecutive games; and a talented, gritty group of reserves that included Robert Horry, Rick Fox, Brian Shaw and Derek Fisher. Veteran John Salley, who has four rings from three different championship teams, was an excellent practice player and a master of the one-liners that kept his team loose.

But the enduring image of this team will be that of O'Neal, an unstoppable force under the basket who has taken his rightful place among the game's greatest players, if not its greatest philosophers and playwrights.

"From now on, I am no longer 'The Big Aristotle,'" he decreed. "I want to be known as 'The Big Shakespeare,' because it was Shakespeare who said, 'Some men are born great, some achieve greatness and some have greatness thrust upon them.'"

After leading the Lakers to "The Big Title," O'Neal can now relate, even when it comes to helping form pop culture. Among the thousands of signs along the parade route, many read, "Bling Bling," which O'Neal said was the sound made by the light bouncing off an NBA championship ring. As a man who once produced a rap CD that went platinum but never was able to win a title in his primary profession of basketball, it was a sound that was not only rhythmic but also rewarding.

Chapter Two

SHAQ

It was a union made by the basketball gods, straight out of Laker Blue Heaven: Phil "Coach of Zen" Jackson and Shaquille "Man of Steel" O'Neal.

The former Chicago Bulls coach with the six championship rings and the superstar with a hunger to start collecting them hit it off instantly in a summer soul session, not long after the Lakers had lured the cerebral Jackson to Los Angeles with a five-year contract.

O'Neal

"He kept it real simple. He said, 'I want you to dominate. I want you to rebound, I want you to score, I want you to play defense. I want you to block shots.'"

Shaq, the mini-conglomerate, happened to be in Montana on unrelated business. He asked a local for the whereabouts of Jackson's ranch, and suddenly he was there, beginning a relationship that would reap immediate and dramatic benefits.

"He's the white version of my father," O'Neal would say months later, 1999-2000 having turned into his dream season. "I do something spectacular, he sits there and goes, 'So what?' He doesn't let me lose my focus. He stays on me all the time. That's what I like. It's what I need.

"He kept it real simple. He said, 'I want you to dominate. I want you to rebound, I want you to score, I want you to play defense. I want you to block shots.' "

O'Neal was raised by a disciplinarian stepfather, Army Sgt. Phillip Harrison, and a nurturing mother, Lucille Harrison. Shaquille took immediately to Jackson's unique style. It didn't hurt when he saw replicas of six championship trophies in his new coach's Montana

Jackson

log-cabin home that afternoon, glistening in reflection as he approached in a rented boat on a lake.

Jackson began preaching a mantra from Day 1 that was not unfamiliar to O'Neal. Shaq would need to expand his game for the Lakers to win titles. He would have to rebound more passionately and defend with increased commitment. The points would always come; Shaq was an offensive machine that would not stop functioning under almost any condition.

What he needed to do, in order to take the dramatic next step, was make his teammates better. It's something Jackson had done with Michael Jordan in Chicago, after His Airness had gone six ring-less seasons, and now it would be Shaq's mission, in his eighth season.

Mission accomplished.

"He's the white version of my father," O'Neal would say months later, 1999-2000 having turned into his dream season. "I do something spectacular, he sits there and goes, 'So what?' He doesn't let me lose my focus. He stays on me all the time. That's what I like. It's what I need."

It was West who had signed O'Neal after an exhaustive free agency courtship, and it was West who predicted during training camp this would be Shaq's MVP season after watching Jackson introduce his triangle offense.

O'Neal's selection as the league's near-unanimous Most Valuable Player – he missed by one vote, the closest anyone had ever come – was confirmation of his elevation into the land not just of the giants, but of the greats of the sport. He led the league in scoring (29.7 points per game) and in field goal percentage (57.4). That was nothing new; he'd been there, done that. What was new was his production in the other areas. He was second in rebounding (13.6 per game) and third in blocked shots (3.03 per game). He dished out more assists (3.8 per game) than ever before. In the Defensive Player of the Year balloting, O'Neal finished second to Miami's Alonzo Mourning. His selection to the NBA All-Defensive Second Team was his first appearance on an all-defensive unit.

The conductor of Showtime in the '80s, minority club owner Magic Johnson, sat courtside for many of O'Neal's performances, rising to applaud along with the rest of the STAPLES Center patrons. The most memorable show came on Shaq's 28th birthday, March 6, when he registered a career-high 61 points against the Clippers.

"Shaq has always been a great scorer," Magic said. "But this season, he became a great defensive player. He became a complete player. It made all the difference in the world."

This was the O'Neal the Lakers envisioned when they signed him as a free agent in the summer of '96, as the former Orlando Magic centerpiece was preparing to help the U.S. win the gold medal at the Summer Olympics in Atlanta.

"Shaquille had an incredible season," said Jerry West, the Lakers' Executive Vice President of Basketball Operations. "He played about as well as I've seen a big man play in this league."

It was West who had signed O'Neal after an exhaustive free agency courtship, and it was West who predicted during training camp this would be Shaq's MVP season after watching Jackson introduce his triangle offense.

From the start, it was clear the triangle, orchestrated by venerable assistant coach Tex Winter, was ideally suited to O'Neal's vast repertoire of talents.

"The emphasis here is more on Shaq because of his ability to score in the post for us," Winter said. "At Chicago, it was more of a perimeter, jump-shooting attack. We wanted to take advantage of Michael and Scottie [Pippen], their abilities. Here, we're going inside more – and Shaq has responded."

Jackson made it clear from the moment he arrived that this would be Shaquille's team, that it would rise and fall with him. The responsibility fit O'Neal as comfortably as one of his tailored suits.

MVP SHAQUILLE O'NEAL

29.7
POINTS PER GAME

57.4
FIELD GOAL PERCENTAGE

13.6
REBOUNDS PER GAME

3.03
BLOCKED SHOTS

3.8
ASSISTS PER GAME

61
CAREER-HIGH POINTS

O'NEAL'S SELECTION AS THE LEAGUE'S NEAR-UNANIMOUS MOST VALUABLE PLAYER – HE MISSED BY ONE VOTE, THE CLOSEST ANYONE HAD EVER COME

Livin' Large

Among other cars, Shaq prizes the Bentley convertible when he gets out on the town. Never the shy one, Shaq loves to see and be seen. If ever there was a match made in heaven, it is Shaq and Hollywood.

Shaq To The Hoop

When he has that look, a couple of steps and is on the way to the basket, the wise move is to get out of the way. "I feel sorry for anybody who has to guard him," said John Salley. "No one can do anything with him. It's up to him whether he's tired or doesn't feel like dominating, which is very rare. You have to foul him, because if you don't, you lose teeth, ribs."

"We create as much operating room as we can for Shaq. We know they're going to be doubling him when they can, and he's done a good job of kicking the ball out, fanning it out. That allows our shooters to get open looks.

Tex Winter — *Assistant Coach, Los Angeles Lakers*

31.5	30.1	27.5	27.4	27.0
MICHAEL **JORDAN**	WILT **CHAMBERLAIN**	SHAQUILLE **O'NEAL**	ELGIN **BAYLOR**	JERRY **WEST**

ALL-TIME SCORERS – POINTS PER GAME

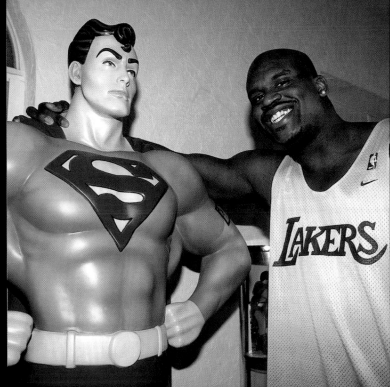

Shaq Block

The path to the NBA championship literally went through O'Neal and the Lakers this season. As Vlade Divac of the Kings – along with the rest of the league – found out, O'Neal's long arms proved a perpetual roadblock along that thoroughfare.

"Shaquille played at such a high level all year," Jackson said. "Everybody knew he could score. But the whole aspect of his game – passing, rebounding, assists, blocked shots, turnovers – when he took those things as indicators of his ability to work within the team and the system, I think that was really another growth step for him. It made this an MVP season."

O'Neal entered his eighth season as the league's fourth all-time scorer at 27.1 points per game, right between Lakers legends Elgin Baylor (27.4) and West (27.0). At the end, he climbed over Baylor into third, at 27.5, trailing only Michael Jordan and Wilt Chamberlain. Fine company, indeed, for the big man from Louisiana State University.

As great a force as O'Neal has been, though, his critics continued to point out he hadn't won a title and hadn't even made it to the Finals since his third season with the Magic, when Orlando was swept by Houston. His first three seasons in L.A. ended in bitter

playoff defeats at the hands of Utah (twice) and San Antonio – not that O'Neal needed to be reminded.

"I'm trying to be focused, trying to bring my 'A' game every night," he said. "I'm getting older. My window is getting slimmer and slimmer."

Which takes us back to Jackson.

"Phil brings something different for Shaquille to deal with," said Lakers' General Manager Mitch Kupchak. "It's an approach he hasn't seen before. Phil's a different guy, with his Indian artifacts, the books and philosophies. It's a fresh approach for a guy who's been in the league for a while.

"Shaquille knows Phil's not going anywhere. He's going to be here. If you remove all the variables, you become clear on the whole picture."

Central to Hollywood's favorite picture are the director and his marquee star, the Coach of Zen and the Man of Steel.

Chapter Three

KOBE

John Salley, as a member of the Detroit Pistons in the '80s and early '90s, imposed his share of "Jordan Rules" on His Airness during the intense rivalry between the Pistons and Chicago Bulls. Later, Salley joined forces with Jordan on Michael's fourth championship journey, with the '96 Bulls.

Coming to the Lakers in 1999-2000 as Shaquille O'Neal's backup, Salley became acquainted with the prince who would be king. Is Kobe Bryant the next Jordan, as widely advertised?

REBOUNDS PER GAME **6.3**

4.9 **ASSISTS PER GAME**

22.5 **POINTS PER GAME**

"I will say this about Kobe: He got a head start on Michael, coming into the league out of high school, and he has a better team around him than Michael had. Kobe works as hard as Michael. He reads everything about Michael and is learning from Michael's mistakes and his abilities."

John Salley

SHOTS BLOCKED PER GAME

0.94

1.61

STEALS PER GAME

"The best thing about it is that Kobe is the next Kobe Bryant," Salley said. "Michael Jordan had to get it out of everyone's mind that he was the next Julius Erving. Kobe is making it as his own person, on his own terms.

"He wants to be the greatest player ever to play. Maturity has made a difference in him, a huge difference. He sees things differently now. He has a coach who believes in him, but who pulls him back – not to restrict his natural ability – but to teach him to get all the points of the game."

Bryant, 21, was an apt pupil. After missing the first 15 games of the season with a broken right hand, Kobe went quickly to work, helping Shaquille O'Neal drive the Lakers to 20 victories in their next 21 games.

By season's end, Kobe had career highs in scoring (22.5 points per game, 12th in the league), rebounds (6.3 per game) and assists (4.9 per game). He also led the team in steals (1.61 per game) and was third in blocked shots (0.94 per game). His tremendous defense on a variety of scorers, from point guards to small forwards, was recognized when he was selected to the NBA All-Defensive First Team.

"Michael Jordan is the best competitor I've ever seen," Sacramento Kings guard Jon Barry said. "Kobe is the second-best. He's the whole package – and he keeps getting better all the time. If you let him have free run in an offense like Allen Iverson or Vince Carter, he'd average 35, at least. You can't stop the guy."

Salley agreed, with a qualifier.

"In another offense, he'd probably be like Allen Iverson," Salley said. "A lot more shots, a lot more points. But it'd ruin his body. It hurt Larry Bird, but it helped Magic Johnson, having Kareem [Abdul-Jabbar] in the middle, like Kobe has Shaq. You can't win a championship by yourself. Every great player needs somebody else.

"I will say this about Kobe: He got a head start on Michael, coming into the league out of high school, and he has a better team around him than Michael had. Kobe works as hard as Michael. He reads everything about Michael and is learning from Michael's mistakes and his abilities.

"He has potential times 10. All he has to do is take care of his body, and he can do whatever he wants to do."

Said Phil Jackson, "He reminds me a lot of Michael, and there aren't too many players who have ever done that. Michael had some of the greatest confidence and self-worth I have ever seen. After a bad game, he would not hold himself to failure and would come back and have a great game. Kobe has that kind of confidence in himself."

The Jordan comparisons have been inevitable from the moment the public began to watch the teenager from Lower Merion High School in Ardmore, Pa., outside Philadelphia, soar for the Lakers. It started in 1996, the same season O'Neal arrived in Los Angeles.

Kobe arrived courtesy of Charlotte in a draft-day swap that sent veteran center Vlade Divac to the Hornets.

Step by step, leap by leap, Bryant has emerged as one of the sport's most spectacular and most popular performers. Voted onto the West starting lineup for the 1998 All-Star Game in his second season, the youngest ever to achieve the distinction at 19, Kobe staged a memorable duel with Jordan. He became an All-Star starter again in 2000.

His abilities may be Jordanesque, but it was another M.J. who influenced Kobe most. Growing up, he wanted to be like Magic Johnson.

"Magic was my favorite player as a kid, besides my dad, of course," said Kobe. "I tried to do all the stuff he was doing back in those days when the Lakers were winning championships. I loved the way Magic got everybody involved in the game – his teammates, fans, everybody."

Kobe's father, Joe "Jelly Bean" Bryant, was a Magic kind of player, without the same results. Joe played for three NBA teams (Philadelphia, San Diego and Houston) across eight seasons before setting off for Europe. Growing up in Italy, Kobe developed his skills by playing against Joe's teammates. Meanwhile, Kobe studied Magic and other greats of the time on film sent over by friends and family members.

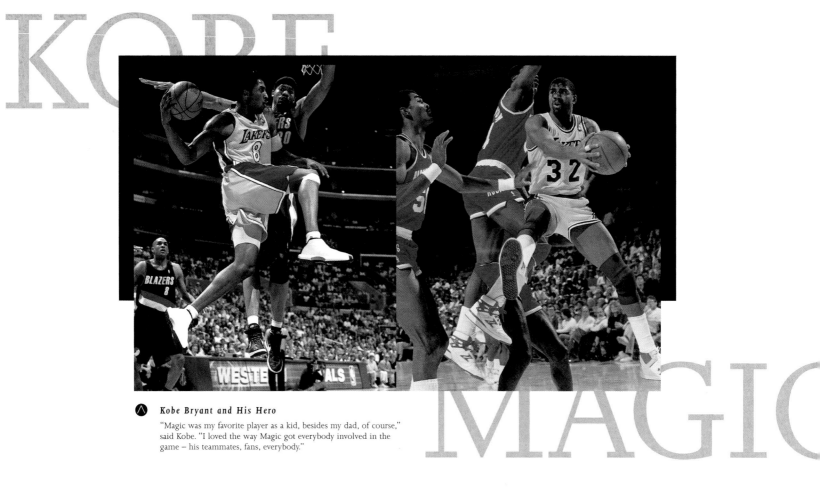

Kobe Bryant and His Hero

"Magic was my favorite player as a kid, besides my dad, of course," said Kobe. "I loved the way Magic got everybody involved in the game – his teammates, fans, everybody."

"He reminds me a lot of Michael, and there aren't too many players who have ever done that."

Phil Jackson

His fourth season was Bryant's best, by leaps and bounds. If he keeps striving, keeps soaring, there are no earthly limits to where the Fresh Prince of L.A. can take his game.

"This is all I ever wanted to do, all I ever wanted
to be. I play for the challenge, to win, to
be the best I can be. That's what drives me."

Kobe Bryant

"What's most impressive about this young man are his desire, his work ethic, his
competitive nature. He comes to the arena at 4:30, before anybody is here, and works
on his game alone. He has incredible skills and the desire to be a great player.

"We're extremely happy with Kobe's development — and we think he's going
to keep improving. You haven't seen the best of Kobe yet."

Jerry West

the TEAM

Just as Michael Jordan and Scottie Pippen could not have done it alone in Chicago, Shaquille O'Neal and Kobe Bryant have required support from a variety of sources in making their Lakers the class of the NBA.

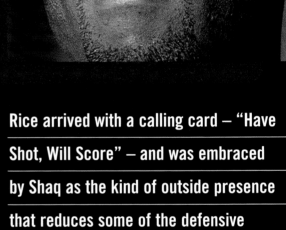

Rice arrived with a calling card – "Have Shot, Will Score" – and was embraced by Shaq as the kind of outside presence that reduces some of the defensive pressure in the paint.

RICE

Glen Rice

He would be a shooting star in most other places, but Glen Rice had to sacrifice personal glory in exchange for winning an NBA title. Clearly, it was a good trade.

"We've got a lot of guys who can play on this team," O'Neal said. "It's up to me and Kobe to get everybody involved. That's when we're a good team."

That simple statement suggests O'Neal is as insightful as he is dominant. When the Lakers are flowing, all their parts functioning smoothly and intensely within the triangle offense and at the defensive end, they are a great team, a model for how to play the game unselfishly.

"All great teams need three reliable offensive weapons," Mitch Kupchak said. "We are lucky to have three in Shaq, Kobe and Glen Rice. We have three people defenses have to be aware of at all times."

Rice, 33, has been one of the NBA's most respected marksmen since his arrival in 1989, the same year he led Michigan to the NCAA championship with one of the greatest individual performances in tournament history. After spending his first nine seasons scoring big numbers for teams (Miami and Charlotte) that lacked

the ingredients to contend for a title, Rice welcomed the trade to the Lakers last season. Charlotte sent Rice, J.R. Reid and B.J. Armstrong to Los Angeles in exchange for Eddie Jones and Elden Campbell.

Rice arrived with a calling card – "Have Shot, Will Score" – and was embraced by Shaq as the kind of outside presence that reduces some of the defensive pressure in the paint. "I came here to try to win a title," Rice said. "When I asked Charlotte to trade me, that was the reason. It was a great thrill [coming to L.A.]. I couldn't wait to play with these guys."

Struggling at times to find shots in the triangle without the benefit of the screens that had freed him up in Charlotte and Miami and expressing his frustration at being the third option, Rice still managed to average 15.9 points in 1999-2000, shooting 43 percent from the field, 36.7 from the three-point line and a team-best 87.4 from the foul line. "Even when he's not scoring in big numbers," Kupchak said, "you have to honor Glen's presence with a defender, and that helps Shaq."

HARPER HORRY GREEN FOX HARPER HORRY G

Rounding out the starting five were a pair of old hands – Ron Harper and A.C. Green – who were brought to Los Angeles to provide leadership and toughness. Harper had been Jordan's backcourt running mate in Chicago on three title teams, and he seemed to be the ideal fit with Bryant. An extension of Jackson on the floor, with what amounted to assistant coaching freedoms, Harper was rough on Kobe at times, trying to make him understand the sacrifices required of champions. "Harp gives me a comfortable feeling, just seeing him out there," Jackson said.

Green, less vocal by nature, led by example – by force of commitment and desire. He is the most durable performer in NBA history with a streak of 1,110 consecutive regular-season games played.

Green reminded Los Angeles fans why he had been so popular as a

Ron Harper
Ron Harper brought three championship rings with him from Chicago, and inspired the Lakers to never throw in the towel.

Rick Fox
Like many of his fellow reserves, Rick Fox was willing to forego individual goals – and absorb plenty of punishment in the paint – to get his hands on the NBA's holy grail.

young Lakers Showtimer during his first eight seasons in the league (1985-93). There were bigger, faster, stronger power forwards in the league, but none worked harder or gave more selflessly than Green, who started all 82 games in 1999-2000. "A.C. was tremendous, everything we brought him here to be," said Jerry West.

Robert Horry served as Green's tag-team partner at power forward. Few teams have the luxury of a talent such as Horry coming off the bench and making things happen. The athletic, 6-10 Horry was a starter for the two-time champion Houston Rockets, blending beautifully with Hakeem Olajuwon. Joining forces with O'Neal, Horry fit right in, hitting pressure shots from distance, passing expertly, defending with passion and rebounding fiercely. "Coming off the bench is just fine with me," Horry said. "A.C. and I are very different, but together, I think, we give the team a lot of energy and production."

Rick Fox supported Rice as ably as Horry backed Green. Another versatile veteran with toughness, experience and a smooth outside stroke, Fox willingly sublimated his considerable talents for the greater good.

A.C. Green
A.C. Green rarely needed help from a friend when it came to extending his NBA record of durability to 1,110 career regular-season games, as well as providing veteran leadership without peer. "I can't look to anyone else to do that," he said.

Robert Horry
Robert Horry came to the Lakers after helping the Rockets win two titles in Houston. He gave the Lakers experience at power forward, as well as playoffs savvy going into the NBA Finals: "If you don't know what's at stake now," he said, "you need to be checked into a mental hospital."

FISHER

Derek Fisher

Always willing to sustain floor burns for the good of the team, Fisher was a relentless competitor.

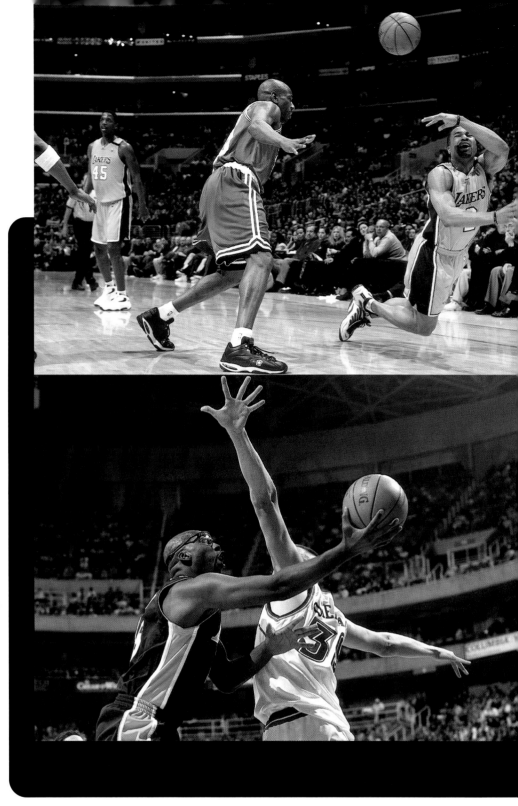

SALLEY

John Salley

Although playing limited minutes, John Salley added a veteran presence and championship experience in the locker room. Retired for three years, Salley returned with three championship rings – two from the Detroit Pistons and one while he was with the Chicago Bulls.

Which was also the common bond of the backcourt reserves — Brian Shaw and Derek Fisher. Shaw, calling on his vast experience in Boston, Miami, Orlando, Golden State and Philadelphia, signed with the Lakers after being released by Houston.

Shaw became best known for his perfect lobs to O'Neal, his former teammate with the Magic, creating what became known as the Shaw-Shaq Redemption. He also played tough defense and ran the team intelligently. "Brian has been a very important player for us with his knowledge and versatility," Jackson said. "And Derek brings a toughness and intelligence that every ballclub needs."

> *"We have a lot of experienced players on this team who keep us younger guys in line. You have to have that nice blend to be a great team."*
>
> Kobe Bryant

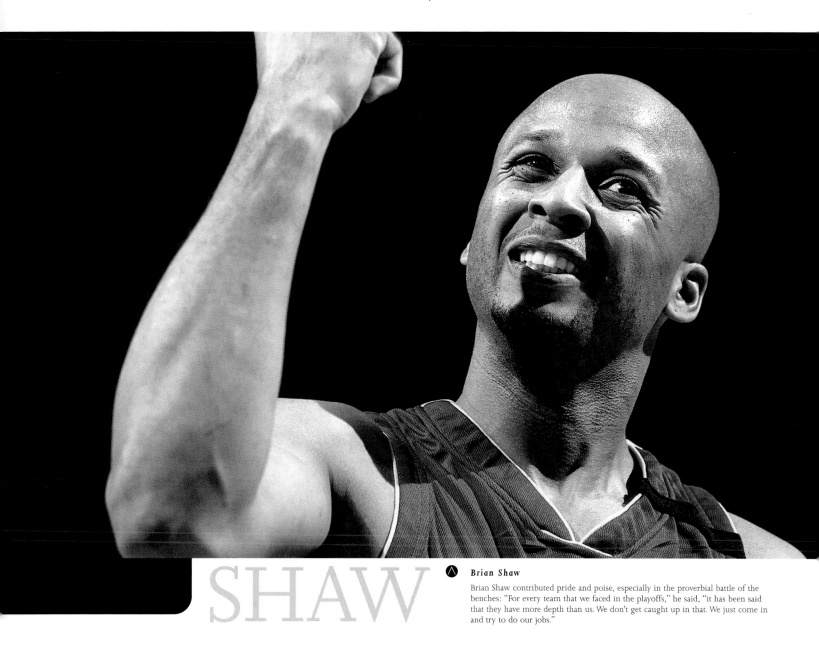

SHAW

Brian Shaw

Brian Shaw contributed pride and poise, especially in the proverbial battle of the benches: "For every team that we faced in the playoffs," he said, "it has been said that they have more depth than us. We don't get caught up in that. We just come in and try to do our jobs."

Fisher, in his fourth season, came off the bench behind Harper with his signature hustle, diving after loose balls, drawing numerous charges and freely giving up his muscular body for the team. He's a fine passer who can make the open jumper while defending the league's ultra-swift small guards.

John Salley, out of the league for three years to pursue interests in the media, showed he was capable of mixing it up in relief of Shaq in the post. Just as important, Salley, twice a champion with Detroit and once with Jackson in Chicago, brought wisdom and humor to the troupe, taking a special interest in O'Neal.

Travis Knight also delivered important backup minutes up front, with rookies Devean George and John Celestand showing flashes of good things to come. Second-year small guard Tyronn Lue was limited to just eight appearances after undergoing knee surgery.

With the focus on the three stars, none of the role players registered impressive individual statistics. But the only numbers that mattered to these guys were 67-15 — leading to home-court advantage throughout the playoffs — to say nothing of 19, 16 and 11, the unprecedented winning streaks assembled by the 1999-2000 Lakers.

PHIL

Chapter Five

Coach Phil Jackson

When Jackson took a stand to make a point, the Lakers were compelled to listen. As Shaquille O'Neal said, "I just did what I was asked to do."

The Men Behind Zen

When Jackson came to Los Angeles he brought (left to right) dependable assistants Frank Hamblen, Jim Cleamons and Tex Winter, and kept longtime Lakers assistant Bill Bertka (behind Hamblen and Cleamons).

When he signed with the Lakers for five seasons, Phil Jackson knew he had two great talents in Shaquille O'Neal and Kobe Bryant and a man who had been a proven scorer in the NBA for years in Glen Rice. The rest of the cast was a mystery. Jackson wasn't very charitable when he took his first look at his new team. This group, he quickly concluded, was not the Chicago Bulls of Michael Jordan and Scottie Pippen.

"There were times when I didn't know really if we had all that it took as a basketball team," Jackson would admit months later.

During what turned out to be a spectacular regular season and playoff run that ended with the Lakers winning the title, he found out that his team indeed had the talent, determination and inner strength to win a title. That performance was Jackson's wordless response to his own critics, those who had suggested that anybody could have rolled out the balls and won six titles in eight seasons with Jordan and Pippen. The Lakers' brain trust imagined great things when they lured Jackson out of a one-year retirement to come to Los Angeles, but they never envisioned it happening so quickly.

Jackson learned the game under Bill Fitch, his college coach at the University of North Dakota, where he was a two-time Division II All-America player, and the legendary Red Holzman, who coached the Knicks when Jackson broke into the NBA in 1967. Jackson spent the first 11 of his 13 NBA seasons in a New York uniform. He was injured when the Knicks won the title in 1970 but was a valued backup forward for the 1973 champions.

He now has won titles with two teams and has a collection of eight championship rings as a coach and player. Not bad for a guy who began his head coaching career with the Albany Patroons of the Continental Basketball Association in 1982, having cut his coaching teeth as an assistant for three seasons (including two as a player-assistant coach) with the New Jersey Nets.

His success in Los Angeles is largely attributed to his adapting the offense to take advantage of the O'Neal. In early think-tank sessions with longtime assistants Tex Winter, Frank Hamblen and Jim Cleamons, along with Lakers holdover Bill Bertka, Jackson quickly deduced that Winter's triangle offense could be modified somewhat to feature Shaq at the apex. In Chicago, it had flowed through the hands of Jordan and Pippen on the perimeter.

It worked spectacularly as Jackson, the celebrated practitioner of Zen, directed the Lakers to a 67-15 record, which is only surpassed by the 1971-72 championship team that won 33 in a row en route to a 69-13 record and league title. "This has been a fairy-tale season for us," Lakers owner Dr. Jerry Buss said, "and I think you have to give a lot of the credit to Phil Jackson. The Lakers have evolved into a different team under Phil. They have a cohesiveness and motivation that was lacking before. I think you can attribute such a change to Phil's coaching. He's done just a great, great job."

jackson

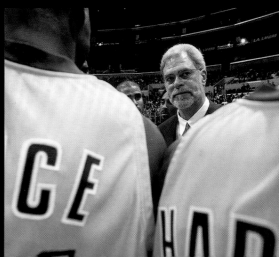

the SEASON

In October and early November, as the new coaching staff became acquainted with an unfamiliar group of athletes, there were no visible signs that the Lakers would emerge as the NBA's dominant team by December and carry it through a remarkable season of accomplishment.

⌂ Kobe Bryant
Kobe Bryant started the season on the bench, but he couldn't be contained for long.

⌂ Glen Rice
Glen Rice exulting after a timely three-pointer was a common thread through the Lakers' successful season.

Expectations, in fact, had bottomed out after Kobe Bryant suffered a broken right hand during the preseason. He was sidelined for the first 15 games and the team struggled with the offensive scheme implemented by Phil Jackson. Assistant coach Tex Winter's triangle attack, which had flowed so smoothly in Chicago all through the 1990s, looked like the Bermuda Triangle in Los Angeles.

"I was telling people that if we were .500 going into January," General Manager Mitch Kupchak said, "I'd be happy." Imagine how Kupchak felt when the Lakers entered the new year 25-5, leading the Pacific Division on their way to a 16-game winning streak.

In a word – Kupchak's – "ecstatic."

The season had opened with a surprising victory in Utah, fueled by Shaquille O'Neal's inside dominance and Glen Rice's 28 points. But four nights later, the Lakers were drubbed in Portland, 97-82, after Shaq was ejected with two technical fouls. Critics viewed this as evidence the Trail Blazers were the team to beat in the Western Conference. Gradually, however, the uneven spots were smoothed over, a transition helped immensely by Bryant's return to action on December 1.

With the two superstars united in their new system, the Lakers won 20 of their next 21 games. On January 14, their 16-game winning streak was snapped by the Pacers in Indianapolis, leading to a brief spin in which Los Angeles lost six of nine. But then came a 19-game winning streak, longest in the league in 28 seasons. That one ended in Washington on March 16, before the Lakers notched 11 more consecutive victories. From February 4 through April 5, they were 30-1. It was the best run in the league since the 1971-72 Lakers reeled off a record 33 wins in a row.

Rick Fox

When the stars came out in L.A. this season, it was time for Rick Fox and the rest of the Lakers' reserves to shine.

"We got off to a much better start than I ever thought would happen," Jackson said. "Shaq played at such a high level the entire year, and Kobe came in here and there was a mutual adjustment. This was a team that did a lot of chest thumping and stuff. Now they carry themselves with a demeanor that is appropriate for their style of play."

And what was that style? Controlled and precise at the offensive end, intense and unyielding at the defensive end. The season crest-

Shaquille O'Neal

The Man of Steel leaps tall Raptors in a single bound. One-on-five is certainly a mismatch, but when the one is Shaquille O'Neal, it's advantage, Lakers.

Ron Harper

Playing the role of a coach on the floor was one that suited Ron Harper. He was truly adept at teaching younger teammates the NBA way, especially when it comes to putting your finger through a championship ring.

ed with a 90-87 victory in Portland on February 29, fueled by O'Neal and Bryant. It triggered a surge that enabled the Lakers to open up distance on the Trail Blazers in the Pacific Division.

At the heart of everything was O'Neal, whose MVP season left him humbled and grateful.

"I think it registered the fact of his improvement this year as a basketball player, a complete basketball player," Jackson said.

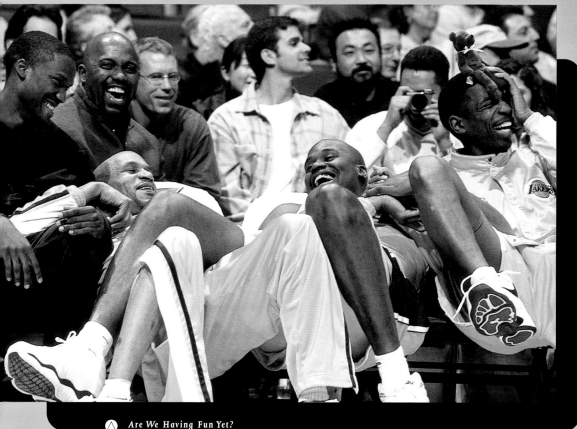

3-2
FIRST ROUND VS. SACRAMENTO

Are We Having Fun Yet?
The Lakers were loose and happy heading into the play-offs. But they were soon surprised by marching Kings who extended Los Angeles to five games.

Green Light
A.C. Green and his band of purple-and-gold mates outmanned and outshined the Suns in the semifinals.

After the brilliant regular season, the Lakers encountered unexpected road obstacles in the first round of the playoffs. Leading the Kings 2-0, the Lakers lost two games at Sacramento before closing out the Kings with a Game 5 rout at STAPLES Center.

In the conference semifinals against Phoenix, Bryant rescued his team in Game 2 at home with a double-clutch jumper over Jason Kidd with 2.6 seconds left for a 97-96 victory. A Game 4 blowout by Phoenix at home forced a return to L.A., where the Lakers rolled to a Game 5 triumph to close out the Suns and force a Western Conference title showdown with Portland.

"This is what everybody wanted," O'Neal said of the clash of titans.

The Lakers almost got more than they wanted. After building a 3-1 series lead, they shockingly lost Game 5 at home and Game 6 in Portland. When the fourth quarter began in Game 7, they were behind by 15 points, but they scored 15 consecutive points while the Blazers recorded 13 consecutive missed shots to escape with a 89-84 victory and a spot in the Finals.

4-1
WESTERN CONFERENCE SEMIFINALS VS. PHOENIX

"We played all season for the home-court advantage.
As long as we win at home, we're all right."

Kobe Bryant

4-3

WESTERN CONFERENCE FINALS VS. PORTLAND

Shaq-A-Blazin'
Implored by fans, the Trail Blazers employed the Hack-A-Shaq strategy, but to no avail. Shaq and Lakers went to the Finals, the Blazers went home.

NBA Finals 2000

Indiana Pacers vs. Los Angeles Lakers

Lakers 104 Pacers 87

The opening act by the Man of Steel and his merry men was an inauspicious one.
Shaquille O'Neal and the Lakers gathered in a circle outside their dressing room door, as they always
do, bounced on the balls of their feet a number of times while bellowing their pregame cheer,
and dashed down the hall and through the tunnel leading to the STAPLES Center floor.
One problem. "The Star-Spangled Banner" was only up to "twilight's last gleaming."
The stunned Lakers stopped short of the floor, retreated to the tunnel and fidgeted until
the national anthem ended. Clearly, they had no answer for Francis Scott Key.

"When you give a guy that big that many shots at the basket, you're not going to win the basketball game."

Austin Croshere

It was O'Neal's first faux pas of the night. It would also be his last. In the grueling seven-game war of attrition won against Portland, the Blazers didn't let Shaq breathe, doubling him, running at him and giving him precious little room to operate. But as Game 1 of the Finals unfolded, O'Neal was able to fill his lungs with fresh air. Operating in the low block with impunity, he was able to do his bidding with little resistance from the overpowered Pacers. Shaq inflicted 43 points and 19 rebounds on the Pacers, who were still trying to get the license number of that Shaqmobile after the game.

Indiana had plenty of other problems, too. One of the Pacers' team buses was caught in the snarl of the L.A. rush hour somewhere between Santa Monica and STAPLES Center, and arrived at the arena only about an hour before tipoff. Clearly, the Lakers' home advantage extends beyond the court.

But if the L.A. traffic slowed the bus, it was nothing compared to the way the Lakers' defense slowed Reggie Miller. While it is true that Miller had some open lanes and looks and simply did not make shots that are usually a given for him, he also was draped by Ron Harper, who spent five years in Chicago and had experience guarding Miller. Indy's bombardier was an uncharacteristic 1-for-16 from the field, which was the sixth-worst performance from the field in the history of the NBA Finals by a player attempting at least 10 shots. And he also had a career playoff-low of a mere seven points.

While Miller was off-target, Shaq was a bull in the eye of the Indiana defense. Over and over, he received the ball in the paint, near the basket, and he was simply devastating.

"We know that's what they're going to do," a weary Davis said, "and he's a heavy load to carry. We just have to do a better job of containing him."

It remained to be seen whether that would be a change in strategy or simply wishful thinking.

As O'Neal met the media after the game, he was asked how he would defend against himself. His reply was made in jest, but the message was clear.

"I wouldn't," he said. "I would just go home."

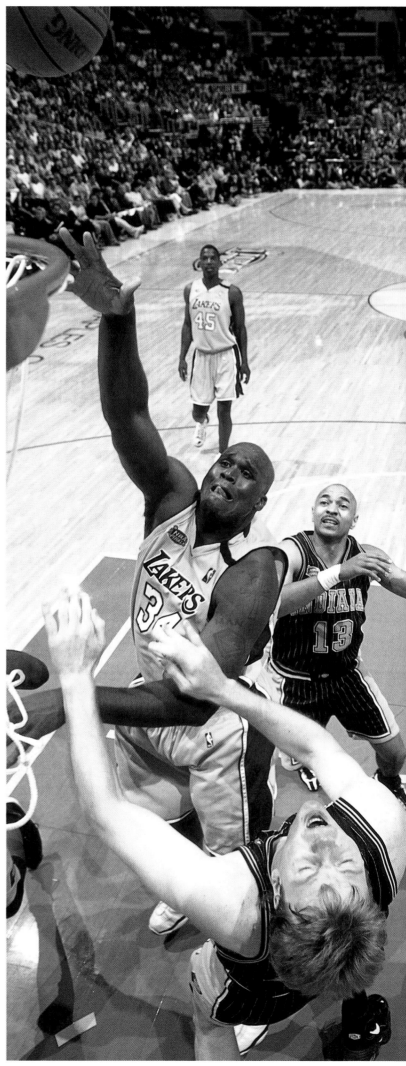

Initially, Indiana tried man-on-man coverage on O'Neal with Rik Smits, (above and opposite image) who could not handle Shaq's brute strength. When the first quarter ended, Shaq had 15 points on 7-of-8 shooting with five rebounds. The task was turned over to All-Star Dale Davis, who fared little better. The same with Sam Perkins. Even when Indiana attempted to double — and later triple — O'Neal, he bulled his way over the Pacers as if they were cardboard cutouts. "We allowed him to do pretty much anything he wanted to," Davis said. Shaq had 21 points at the half, and 31 after three. When Smits was asked if the thought of O'Neal possibly putting up even bigger numbers in Game 2 had crossed his mind, he replied, "It can't. That would be too depressing."

Kobe Bryant is anything but the shy type, but for the better part of Game 1, he played the wallflower to Shaq's laser light show. In the final three quarters, he was 2-for-7 from the field and scored six points. But it was in the waning moments of the first quarter that Bryant put on a move destined for the highest of highlights — a baseline drive that culminated in a rim-rattling, two-handed dunk. The parallel of Bryant sailing gracefully through the air while the landlocked Pacers could do little more than admire his elegance and power would underscore the proceedings on this night.

Despite Shaq's dominance, Indiana managed to stage a pair of spirited uprisings to get within six and two. The Pacers hacked a 17-point deficit to two in the waning moments of the third quarter, and the STAPLES Center crowd, which had been so ebullient early on, was beginning to squirm. But the scene was settled by the Lakers' steady reserves, led by the cool-handed Brian Shaw. With Bird helpless in the background, Shaw came up golden with a three-pointer to help stem the tide. Bryant reappeared, (bottom right) as well, rediscovering his touch with a pair of buckets. Robert Horry and Rick Fox were also heard from, and a 25-10 Los Angeles run let the party begin anew.

The rare forays the Pacers managed into the lane were usually brought to a halt by O'Neal's imposing wingspan, as Travis Best and his cohorts found out time and again. Shaq had three blocks and inhaled 19 rebounds, more than half the total of the entire Indiana team. The Pacers did have openings on the perimeter, but the majority of their launches hit nothing but iron. "Rik Smits had a ton of wide-open looks early and none of them went in," Indiana coach Larry Bird said. "We just didn't make any shots."

All the signs usually point to Reggie Miller, who has made a career of twisting the dagger just when the opponent thinks it's safe to celebrate. Miller, who went to UCLA, held that dagger in his hand for his first Finals game, but he never figured to stumble and fall on it himself. Before the Finals began, Miller proclaimed the Pacers would "shock the world." He wasn't entirely wrong, as he suffered through perhaps the ugliest night of his career: only 1-for-16 from the field with seven points, the sixth-worst shooting performance in NBA Finals history of any player who attempted at least 10 field goals. He scored his only basket with 5:42 left in the third quarter, but exhibiting the true shooter's mentality, vowed to find the openings and knock down the good looks in Game 2. "I'm looking forward to it," he said stoically. "Just one of those off nights, and Friday will be our night."

It had been 13 years since Larry Bird stood on a basketball floor in Los Angeles during the NBA Finals. And that old Celtic pride bubbled forth as Bird brought the Pacers into L.A. for what was, to him, like old times. This was different, though. In the mid-1980s, he could put a gag on Jack Nicholson and the L.A. glitterati with a well-placed three-pointer or two. But the green hightops have since given way to brown oxfords, and Bird's influence was limited to the sideline — which was something that pleased the Lakers.

O'Neal was simply unstoppable all night, but he needed to provide a signature, an exclamation point. He grabbed the pen with 3:05 to play. Beginning high in the lane, he exhibited power as well as grace, as he advanced on Davis before spinning to his right, a move that would make a ballerina's jaw drop. With nothing between him and the basket, O'Neal looked to his left, where Shaw had already floated a pass above the rim. O'Neal left the floor, leaping into space, where he got his right hand on the ball and slammed it through the hole. As O'Neal returned up the floor, he lumbered sideways along the sidelines, striking a pose for the ages. It was his final score of the game, as he finished with 43 points and left the game moments later to the strains of the STAPLES Center crowd, howling, "MVP! MVP!"

"The Big Aristotle," as he calls himself, attracts crowds wherever he goes. And even in the star-glutted environs of Los Angeles, where double-takes are as rare as rain, Shaquille O'Neal turns heads. His world is a non-stop carnival, replete with toys and gadgets — a cavalcade of sights and sounds. His favorite postgame hangout is the massive game room in the basement of his home, where he often pretends to spar with a life-size statue of Bruce Lee. But in the minutes counting down to taking the largest stage in his larger-than-life 28 years, he chose the solitude and sanctity of the Lakers' dressing room, using the time to cram in a few more moments of game film.

O'Neal was asked how he
would defend against himself.
"I wouldn't," he said.
"I would just go home."

Game 1

PACERS						REBOUNDS								
PLAYER	POS	MIN	FGM-A	3PM-A	FTM-A	OFF	DEF	TOT	AST	PF	ST	TO	BS	PTS
Rose	F	36	5-12	2-3	0-0	0	2	2	2	4	0	3	0	12
Davis	F	28	4-5	0-0	1-2	3	5	8	0	3	1	0	1	9
Smits	C	20	5-12	0-0	2-2	0	5	5	0	6	1	4	2	12
Miller	G	41	1-16	0-3	5-5	0	2	2	4	1	1	0	0	7
Jackson	G	28	6-8	2-3	4-5	1	4	5	7	3	0	0	0	18
Croshere		26	6-7	0-1	4-7	1	5	6	0	3	0	3	1	16
Perkins		21	1-5	1-3	2-2	0	2	2	0	3	1	1	0	5
Best		19	2-7	0-0	0-0	1	1	2	2	0	2	1	1	4
McKey		12	0-1	0-1	0-0	0	4	4	0	0	0	1	0	0
Mullin		4	0-0	0-0	0-0	0	0	0	1	0	0	1	0	0
Tabak		3	0-0	0-0	0-0	0	0	0	0	0	0	0	0	0
Bender		2	2-3	0-0	0-0	0	0	0	0	0	0	0	0	4
TOTAL		240	32-76	5-14	18-23	6	30	36	16	23	6	14	5	87
			(42.1)	(35.7)	(78.3)				Team Rebs: 7		Total TO: 14 (19 Pts)			

LAKERS						REBOUNDS								
PLAYER	POS	MIN	FGM-A	3PM-A	FTM-A	OFF	DEF	TOT	AST	PF	ST	TO	BS	PTS
Rice	F	27	1-8	0-2	1-2	1	2	3	1	2	2	2	0	3
Green	F	22	2-6	0-0	0-0	1	4	5	1	1	0	0	0	4
O'Neal	C	44	21-31	0-0	1-6	6	13	19	4	2	0	2	3	43
Bryant	G	38	6-13	0-2	2-2	0	3	3	5	4	1	2	2	14
Harper	G	21	4-6	1-2	3-5	1	0	1	5	2	0	1	0	12
Fox		24	3-4	1-1	4-4	0	4	4	2	1	1	1	0	11
Horry		23	3-5	0-0	0-0	1	3	4	2	4	3	1	1	6
Fisher		19	2-4	1-1	0-0	1	1	2	2	2	2	1	0	5
Shaw		18	2-9	0-4	0-0	1	4	5	3	0	0	1	0	4
Salley		3	0-0	0-0	0-0	0	0	0	0	0	0	0	0	0
Knight		1	1-2	0-0	0-0	2	0	2	0	1	0	0	0	2
George		DNP - Did not dress												
TOTAL		240	45-88	3-12	11-19	14	34	48	25	19	9	11	6	104
			(51.1)	(25.0)	(57.9)				Team Rebs: 9		Total TO: 12 (11 Pts)			

Lakers 111 Pacers 104

As the curtain arose on Game 2, Reggie Miller entered stage right, carrying the weight of his own personal guarantee on his rangy shoulders. After his Game 1 clunker, Miller had promised that he would cease moonlighting as a bricklayer and return to his more familiar vocations of villain, sharpshooter and scoreboard light spinner. When Game 2 opened, the stars appeared to be realigned in Miller's universe. Indeed, the atmospheric conditions inside STAPLES Center revealed a subtle air of apprehension as Jack, Dyan, Dustin, Magic and the other beautiful people at courtside grimaced as Miller hit his first shot of the night and scored six of the Pacers' first eight points.

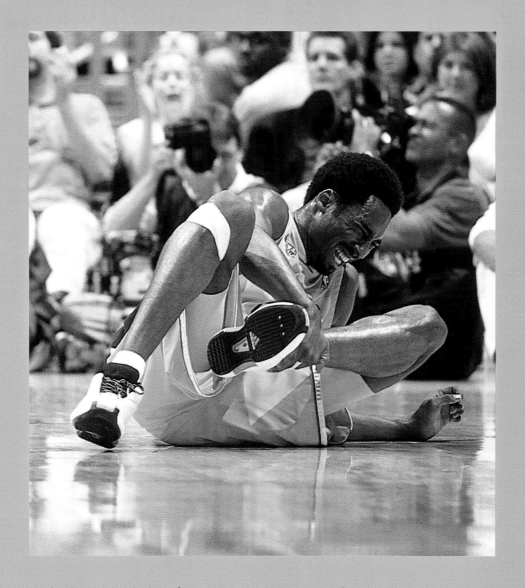

The concern turned to horror shortly thereafter. With 3:26 remaining in the first quarter, Kobe Bryant drained a 17-footer from the right wing as the partisan crowd roared its approval. That was quickly followed by a gasp when Bryant's left foot landed atop the foot of the Pacers' Jalen Rose. Bryant's ankle turned over grotesquely and he crumbled to the floor and had to be helped to the Lakers' dressing room. He would not return.

The Lakers, however, refused to crumble. While Miller scored 21 points, his last basket came on a two-handed dunk with 4:41 remaining in the third period. Meanwhile, Shaquille O'Neal strapped the Lakers on his arms of steel and carried them to the victory. When the night began, the record for most free throw attempts in an NBA Finals game was 24. When it ended, it had not been broken by O'Neal, but obliterated. Indiana's fourth-quarter Hack-a-Shaq strategy resulted in O'Neal going to the line a staggering 39 times – more than in any game, playoff or otherwise, in NBA history.

Shaq made only 18 of them, but the Pacers couldn't take advantage. The Lakers, propelled by another display of gaudiness from their 7-1, 315-pound wonder of the world – 40 points and 24 rebounds – prevailed. And Game 2 ended as Game 1 did – with purple and gold confetti cascading from the ceiling, the Laker Girls in their glory, and Randy Newman's "I Love L.A." blaring.

The Lakers were halfway to the Larry O'Brien Trophy, but the next three games would be at Conseco Fieldhouse. And how long would Kobe be out? Could they win without him?

⋀

Bryant's injury was the ultimate cue card for Reggie Miller and the Pacers. The window of opportunity had suddenly opened wide, and all the necessary elements for an Indiana comeback had fallen in the Pacers' laps. Miller was effective early on, finding the looks and hitting the holes he had not two nights before; he had eight points after one quarter, more than he scored in all of Game 1. But with a spot in NBA Finals lore all but put aside for him, Miller was strangely silent. In the fourth quarter, which is usually Miller Time, he got only two shots and his only two points of the period came on free throws. "We had a golden opportunity tonight that slipped through our fingers," he said.

⋖

Although the Pacers were more aggressive at going to the basket, ultimately the Lakers still had the ultimate answer in Shaq.

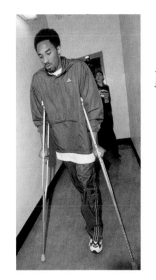

"The guys came in the locker room and said that they were going to step up, they were going to make this thing happen. I believed them."

Kobe Bryant

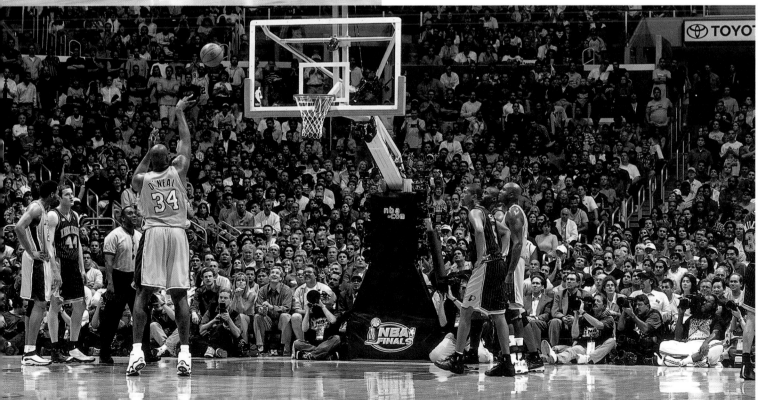

◀

After injuring his ankle, Bryant tried to get up and run back downcourt, but found the pain too great. He immediately was taken to the locker room, where he watched the remainder of the game while getting treatment. X-rays were negative, but Bryant would spend the next several days on crutches. "It was just pain," Bryant said. "It was just flat-out pain." On a record-setting night, Shaq (below) went to the line 39 times, making only 18. But he was 9-of-16 in the fourth quarter, which did help L.A.'s cause.

"We played the first two months without Kobe. It's not something we like. But it's something we know how to deal with."

Rick Fox

Throughout his career, there has been one void preventing Shaquille O'Neal from being complete, and he has even said it himself in the past: "The only places I haven't won are in college … and the NBA." It is widely understood that to truly be considered one of the great ones, it is necessary to fill that void with a championship ring. And for the first time, O'Neal's name was being mentioned in the same breath as those of Chamberlain, Abdul-Jabbar and Russell. The Pacers did a better job of applying pressure to O'Neal in Game 2, but once again, it was apparent Indiana was using popguns to try and stop a tank. When Shaq was alone (above), he was unstoppable. And when the Pacers converged en masse, he also was unstoppable.

"He just looked like a man among boys."

Austin Croshere, on Shaquille O'Neal

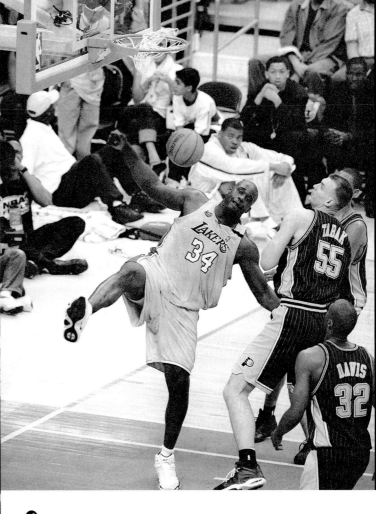

He made a habit of proclaiming himself none of the first several offensive options for the Pacers, but for the second time in as many Finals games, Austin Croshere came off the bench to provide Indiana with energy. Even more appreciated by the Pacers were the season-high 24 points he delivered in Game 2, as he was a force down low, fighting off crowds of Lakers defenders and finishing powerful trips through the paint to supplant Miller's 21 points and a team-high 30 from Jalen Rose. Croshere was also a perfect 12-for-12 from the free-throw line.

Although the Pacers double- and triple-teamed Shaq, it ultimately made no difference as he simply overpowered his way to the basket (top). Shaq became only the fourth player in NBA history to have back-to-back games of 40 or more points. The others were Michael Jordan, Rick Barry and Jerry West (who did it twice). Instead of Miller Time, the fourth quarter was hang-your-head time for Miller (top right). With Bryant out, veteran Brian Shaw (right) played 32 minutes. Although he was only 1-of-9 from the field, he had seven assists and played excellent defense.

"I thought he played better tonight than the other night. I thought he was awesome the other night."

Larry Bird, on Shaquille O'Neal

With Bryant reduced to hobbling on crutches in a STAPLES Center hallway, the Lakers were one hero down, and sorely in need of another. And fortunately for L.A., Glen Rice and Ron Harper were both able to squeeze into the same phone booth. The pair scored 21 points apiece — a season-high for Harper, who helped repel the Pacers in the fourth quarter when he drove the lane and kissed a floater off the glass with 8:11 to play, and added four free throws in the final minute to ice it. "Somehow I found some energy," Harper said. "I just came out and did the things I had to do." Rice was particularly lethal from long range, connecting on five of six three-point launches. "A lot of people see me as the third option," Rice said, "and without Kobe, there seems to be more things happening for me out there."

Before the game, O'Neal did his best to capture every moment, even during the mundane routine of taping. As it turned out, Shaq had better luck focusing and clicking in the trainer's room than he did from the free-throw line. Apparently, he did not receive a phone call from his daughter before the game, imploring her daddy to "bend your knees." He was shooting straight, all right — straight at the rim, as his shots continually clanked. He was 2-for-7 from the line after the first quarter, 5-for-17 at the half and 9-for-23 after three. In the final quarter, unable to stop O'Neal any other way, the desperate Pacers turned to Hack-a-Shaq. Indiana took to hugging O'Neal away from the ball and sent him to the line 16 times. He managed to hit nine of those, and the Pacers failed to whittle the Lakers' lead. By the time the final buzzer sounded, Shaq had shattered NBA records for free throws in a half (doing so in both halves) and a game. "If you really play him straight up and make him earn everything he gets, that's how you can get to Shaq," Jalen Rose said, "as opposed to just fouling him and giving him free points." But for the Pacers, neither way was working.

Game 2

PACERS						REBOUNDS								
PLAYER	POS	MIN	FGM-A	3PM-A	FTM-A	OFF	DEF	TOT	AST	PF	ST	TO	BS	PTS
Rose	F	48	10-23	0-1	10-14	1	8	9	1	3	1	2	1	30
Davis	F	34	4-9	0-0	1-1	4	6	10	1	6	0	0	2	9
Smits	C	16	2-6	0-0	0-0	1	1	2	2	5	0	0	0	4
Miller	G	36	7-16	1-5	6-6	0	2	2	4	4	0	0	0	21
Jackson	G	29	2-9	2-7	1-2	0	9	9	8	4	2	1	0	7
Croshere		25	6-15	0-2	12-12	4	2	6	1	4	1	0	2	24
Perkins		24	2-5	2-4	0-0	0	3	3	1	6	1	0	0	6
Best		19	0-3	0-1	2-2	0	1	1	0	1	0	0	0	2
McKey		6	0-1	0-0	1-2	2	1	3	1	2	0	1	0	1
Tabak		3	0-1	0-0	0-0	1	0	1	0	3	0	0	0	0
Mullin		DNP - Coach's Decision												
Bender		DNP - Coach's Decision												
TOTAL		240	33-88	5-20	33-39	13	33	46	19	38	5	4	5	104
			(37.5)	(25.0)	(84.6)					Team Rebs: 13 Total TO: 6 (7 Pts)				

LAKERS						REBOUNDS								
PLAYER	POS	MIN	FGM-A	3PM-A	FTM-A	OFF	DEF	TOT	AST	PF	ST	TO	BS	PTS
Rice	F	35	7-15	5-6	2-2	0	4	4	3	4	0	1	0	21
Green	F	15	2-4	0-0	0-0	3	1	4	1	1	0	1	0	4
O'Neal	C	46	11-18	0-0	18-39	5	19	24	4	5	0	2	3	40
Bryant	G	9	1-3	0-1	0-0	0	1	1	4	1	0	0	1	2
Harper	G	37	8-12	1-2	4-5	0	3	3	6	4	0	3	0	21
Fox		15	2-3	0-0	2-3	1	1	2	0	4	1	1	0	6
Horry		33	2-6	0-2	3-4	1	5	6	5	5	0	1	4	7
Fisher		16	2-4	1-1	1-2	0	0	0	3	1	0	0	0	6
Shaw		32	1-9	0-3	2-2	1	2	3	7	1	1	0	0	4
Salley		1	0-1	0-0	0-0	0	0	0	0	0	1	0	0	0
Knight		1	0-0	0-0	0-0	0	0	0	0	0	0	0	0	0
George		DNP - DNP - Coach's Decision												
TOTAL		240	36-75	7-15	32-57	11	36	47	29	26	3	9	8	111
			(48.0)	(46.7)	(56.1)					Team Rebs: 19 Total TO: 10 (10 Pts)				

| **G a m e 3** – June 11, 2000 |

Pacers 100   Lakers 91

"Really, there's no pressure on them. It's squarely on us and it's up to us to respond."

Reggie Miller, on going home to Conseco Fieldhouse for Game 3

Clearly, there was no reason for the Pacers to hold anything back — not with the danger of falling into a 3-0 abyss staring them in the face. So Miller came to play, and make the Lakers pay with 33 points. After draining a third-quarter three-pointer from the right wing to give Indiana a 76-58 lead, Miller felt the spotlight burning the back of his neck and raised his arms to the rafters while hopping back on defense. Find some shade? Not on this night. "I've got to let it pour out," he said. "I can't play quiet. There's just no way. I play on emotion and excitement. It's always been that way."

As a public service to the geographically challenged, the scoreboard at Conseco Fieldhouse saw fit to note one significant fact prior to Game 3:

"In 49 states, it's just basketball. But this is Indiana."

If the Lakers were aware of anything as they took the court inside the magnificent retro shrine to Indiana's rich basketball heritage, it was this: They weren't in L.A. anymore. The 18,345 sets of lungs enveloping the floor kept reminding them of that for the better part of two hours and 32 minutes.

For effect, the Pacers could have chosen to break out the satin shorts and canvas hightops. But that was not necessary, for they brought their retro game on a night that demanded nothing less — the game that enabled them to build a 36-5 regular season record at the Fieldhouse; the game that allowed them to vanquish Milwaukee, Philadelphia and New York on the road to their first NBA Finals; the game everyone was waiting to see from Reggie Miller.

Forgettable in Game 1 and a fadeout in Game 2, Miller effectively stepped back in time, knowing too well that failure was not an option. Openly admitting, "You probably could have written us off," in the event of a third straight loss to Los Angeles, Miller stepped up and stepped out, hitting for 33 points to slice the Lakers' series lead to 2-1, all the while exhorting the Conseco fans to make even more noise, though that didn't seem possible.

"It always comes down to me," Miller said. "This is my team. I've got to step up and I've got to do everything."

The Lakers played without the injured Kobe Bryant — who spent the night receiving treatment for his sprained left ankle in the team's training room — and to no one's surprise, there was a marked difference in their energy level. Meanwhile, the juiced-up Pacers were notably more efficient running double teams at O'Neal — who still managed 33 points — and limiting the Lakers' dangerous shooters to low-percentage shots on the perimeter.

"We hear a lot of talk about people wondering how long the series is going to be, when L.A. is going to put us out of our misery, and things of that nature," said Jalen Rose, who contributed 21 points to the Pacers' cause. "But we're not going out like that."

> "We hear a lot of talk about people wondering how long the series is going to be, when L.A. is going to put us out of our misery, and things of that nature. But we're not going out like that."
>
> Jalen Rose

In Games 1 and 2, Shaquille O'Neal had his way with the Pacers, and might as well have thrown down a tarp and buckets, so much was he in control of the paint. But in Game 3, the inspired Pacers refused to let O'Neal breathe. They pushed a steady stream of double teams in his direction, and did a better job of keeping him from the shadow of the hoop. He finished with 33 points and 13 rebounds, but it was a much quieter performance than his thunderclaps in his first two outings during the Finals. "I thought we did a better job of at least trying to push him out," Dale Davis said. "I thought we went a little harder tonight."

With the intensity of the pregame introductions still sizzling through the air inside Conseco Fieldhouse, Jalen Rose did his best to keep the temperature high and put the heat on the visiting Lakers. The noise and passion emanating from the crowd was certainly infectious, and Rose kept it going by notching six of the Pacers' first 10 points.

The most consistent Pacer through the first three games of the Finals was not even one of their starters. Once again, Austin Croshere was energetic and effective, particularly during one stretch in the second quarter when Croshere tallied six straight points for Indiana, including a three-pointer. "Our confidence is high," Croshere said. "I think we came out from the beginning and really tried to set the pace instead of following the pace like we did in Los Angeles."

The heavyweights who tilted the scales in the direction of the Pacers were Rik Smits, Dale Davis (above) and Sam Perkins, who combined to help Indiana win the battle of the boards against the Lakers 39-33, and ultimately the game. Davis finished with 12 rebounds — one less than O'Neal — including six in the first quarter. "We figured it would be a key, even before the series started," Smits said. "We said the same thing when we played New York. We need to keep that same kind of effort."

"You can just feel it coming into the building before the game. We talked about it and knew this was going to be a special day."

Mark Jackson

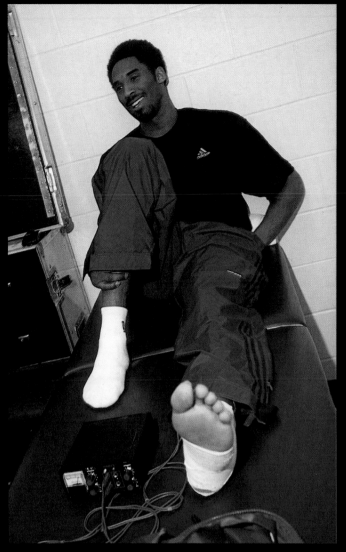

> "We didn't make them fade.
> You have to make a team fade. We got close,
> but not close enough." Rick Fox

Though they didn't have the vast talent of Bryant to bail them out, the Lakers were nearly able to wrest the game from the Pacers' grasp. Los Angeles recorded a 14-5 run to pull within 89-85 with 3:03 to play, thanks to consecutive three-pointers by Rick Fox and Derek Fisher, and a spin move in the post by O'Neal. But in the end, the Lakers were victimized by crucial turnovers — not to mention going 8-for-19 from the free-throw line, including a 3-for-13 line from O'Neal. "I felt we played a pretty good game," Ron Harper said. "It's just that we made some bonehead plays."

> "We knew that they were going to play
> harder at home. They got their fans and they
> play good at home. But we had a chance."

Ron Harper

In every corner of Conseco Fieldhouse, necks craned and eyes squinted in the direction of the Lakers' bench. Where was Kobe Bryant? They were relieved he was nowhere to be seen, as he was receiving treatment for his sprained left ankle in the relative calmness of the visitors' dressing room. He tried to trumpet a clean bill of health to Lakers coach Phil Jackson before the game, but Jackson was unconvinced. "Actually," Jackson said, "he put his shoes on and came in the coaches' room about 35 minutes before game time and said, 'I can go'. And he said, 'I can try it'. I wanted to see him do some lateral slides, and I asked him how it felt. He said, 'It hurts'. I said, 'Well, then, let's save it. We can save this one'. "

Game 3

LAKERS

PLAYER	POS	MIN	FGM-A	3PM-A	FTM-A	OFF	DEF	TOT	AST	PF	ST	TO	BS	PTS
Rice	F	27	3-9	1-3	0-0	0	1	1	1	0	1	2	1	7
Green	F	14	1-2	0-0	2-2	0	1	1	1	3	0	0	0	4
O'Neal	C	47	15-24	0-0	3-13	4	9	13	1	3	2	3	2	33
Harper	G	38	6-14	2-3	0-0	1	4	5	2	2	5	5	1	14
Shaw	G	31	3-10	0-3	0-0	0	5	5	1	4	1	2	0	6
Fox		21	2-4	2-3	1-2	0	0	0	1	5	0	1	0	7
Horry		33	5-8	0-2	0-0	3	4	7	6	4	0	3	0	10
Fisher		27	3-5	2-3	2-2	0	1	1	10	4	0	0	0	10
Knight		2	0-0	0-0	0-0	0	0	0	0	2	0	0	0	0
Bryant		DNP - Did not dress												
Salley		DNP - Coach's Decision												
George		DNP - Coach's Decision												
TOTAL		240	38-76	7-17	8-19	8	25	33	23	27	9	16	4	91
			(50.0)	(41.2)	(42.1)				Team Rebs: 10		Total TO: 17 (25 Pts)			

PACERS

PLAYER	POS	MIN	FGM-A	3PM-A	FTM-A	OFF	DEF	TOT	AST	PF	ST	TO	BS	PTS
Rose	F	45	9-18	0-4	3-3	0	6	6	2	2	1	2	0	21
Davis	F	28	1-5	0-0	0-0	4	8	12	1	6	0	0	0	2
Smits	C	19	3-11	0-0	0-0	3	3	6	0	4	1	1	2	6
Miller	G	46	11-22	2-7	9-9	0	2	2	2	0	1	3	0	33
Jackson	G	27	2-5	1-1	1-2	0	2	2	6	1	2	3	0	6
Croshere		27	4-6	1-1	3-4	0	3	3	0	1	0	0	1	12
Perkins		22	1-4	1-3	0-0	0	4	4	1	2	1	1	0	3
Best		21	5-7	2-2	2-2	1	0	1	2	2	2	1	0	14
McKey		5	0-0	0-0	3-4	1	2	3	0	1	0	1	0	3
Mullin		DNP - Coach's Decision												
Tabak		DNP - Coach's Decision												
Bender		DNP - Coach's Decision												
TOTAL		240	36-78	7-18	21-24	9	30	39	14	19	8	12	3	100
			(46.2)	(38.9)	(87.5)				Team Rebs: 12		Total TO: 13 (17 Pts)			

| Game 4 – June 14, 2000 |

Lakers 120 Pacers 118
(OT)

*"Right now, we're definitely behind the eight-ball at 3-1,
but we've got a little bit of pulse in the heart."* Reggie Miller

For one night, he was probably the most scrutinized person wearing purple shorts in the
blue-and-gold bedecked Conseco Fieldhouse – even more of a curiosity than Shaq. Kobe Bryant had returned for
Game 4 but still was burdened by a gimpy ankle that obviously limited his lateral movement and was not even close to
100 percent. In the first half, he was quiet — six points and little promise that the ankle would allow him to be any better.
But sitting in a sepia-toned background is not Bryant's way. He is style, verve and brilliance, a tsunami of exuberance.
In the second half of Game 4, he was even more. Taking charge, he reminded his team and Lakers fans
what they had missed through the better part of the previous two games.

"I actually dreamed about hitting the game-winning shot at the top of the key. When it was 2.3 seconds left [in regulation], I was like, "Oh, my God, this might happen." Kobe Bryant

"I realize that every great team has a one-two punch and for this team,
Kobe and myself, we are the one-two punch." Shaquille O'Neal

Like the scout in an old western who proclaims it being "too quiet" before taking an arrow in the chest, so it was that Kobe Bryant came out in the third quarter and
single-handedly began piercing holes in the Pacers. He had actually shown a flash of his familiar form in the waning minutes of the first half; covered on a baseline drive
by Dale Davis and Jalen Rose, Bryant somehow had the poise and presence to throw a blind behind-the-back pass to Shaquille O'Neal, who slammed home a thunderous dunk.
It was yet another example of the karma and kismet that exists between the two teammates. Said O'Neal: "We've always had that big-brother, little-brother relationship."

Bryant delivered one of the most extraordinary Finals performances in one of the most memorable Finals games, and that was with O'Neal supplying his usual gargantuan numbers — 36 points and 21 rebounds. After Shaq fouled out in overtime, Bryant took over, hitting eight points, including three of the Lakers' final four buckets, and finished with 28 points to propel the Lakers to a 3-1 series lead.

With 5.9 seconds to play in overtime Bryant twisted free underneath the basket to grab a rebound and put in the winning points. He said it was meant to be — the fulfillment of a vision.

"I actually dreamed about hitting the game-winning shot at the top of the key," he said afterward, clad in a Carolina blue warm-up suit and his omnipresent floppy hat. "When it was 2.3 seconds left [in regulation], I was like, 'Oh my God, this might happen.'"

Reggie Miller was brilliant, scoring 35 points to fuel the impassioned Pacers. As the seconds ticked off in overtime, Miller launched a three-point shot that was within one rotation of going down and tying the series.

But in the end, Bryant's name would be the one on everyone's lips, and in the Pacers' nightmares. In an intense, well played, hotly contested affair, Bryant made the ending one for the ages.

"Their back is now against the wall officially." Phil Jackson

After scoring eight of his team's 16 points in overtime — crowned by what proved to be the winning score when he put back the rebound of a Brian Shaw shot with 5.9 seconds to play — Bryant basked in the role of the hero, reminiscent of another shooting guard that once played for Phil Jackson. Pressure? What's that? "When things get thick, you know, you just look up in the crowd," he said. "Look up at the fans, everybody's waving their towels, it's like a crescendo of cheers. You just lose yourself in the moment. At that time, you don't feel pressure. You're just consumed by the game."

As the fourth quarter unfolded, Indiana would hold Los Angeles without a field goal for a stretch of 4:38, and the Pacers took advantage on the offensive end as well, racking up a 12-2 run to turn an 82-79 deficit into an 89-84 lead. The big shots were back-to-back three-pointers by Reggie Miller and Sam Perkins (right) — the latter so open, all action around him seemed to slow to a crawl and the crowd hushed as he took his time, lined up the three and swished it.

> ## "He's done it so many times for us and we can't expect him to do it every night."
>
> Rik Smits on Reggie Miller

"Happy Trails" was pounding through the loudspeaker at Conseco Fieldhouse, but O'Neal wasn't smiling — not after going over the top of Smits and fouling out of the game with 2:33 remaining in regulation. Still, Shaq did manage to find some solace as he trudged off the floor, courtesy of one very special teammate. "Kobe winked at me and said, 'Don't worry about it, I got it.' He's the hero of the game, and I'm just glad I'm part of this legendary one-two punch."

One of the most significant keys to the Pacers' Game 3 victory was their ability to keep Shaquille O'Neal away from the shadow of the basket. But they were not nearly as effective in Game 4, as O'Neal was a constant presence in the paint. The regular-season MVP continued to campaign for the same honors in the NBA Finals, as he finished with 36 points and 21 rebounds. Perhaps the most notable part of his performance was his free-throw shooting — 10-for-17 from the line, after his dismal 3-for-13 in Game 3. "I realize we let one get away the other day," O'Neal said, "so I was saying to myself all day, 'Just go ahead and make them.' I made most of them tonight."

Bryant came out for the second half spinning and soaring, as he scored the Lakers' first six points of the second half on an 11-foot jumper, a 16-foot jumper and a 6-foot running jumper. A Ron Harper drive and a Glen Rice three-pointer later, Los Angeles gained its first lead of the game. A few minutes later, Bryant served notice of his returned health when he served up a spectacular two-handed dunk on a baseline drive. "You just wait for key moments in the game to attack," he said. "This game wasn't going to be won in the first half. You just kind of pace it out. In the third quarter we needed a little push. I pushed it." But there was more pushing to come.

Outmuscled and victimized by a flurry of fouls in his battle for post position with O'Neal, Rik Smits had his finest game of the series. He started off strong on the offensive end from the opening tip, as he hit his first four shots and had eight points — two less than his total output in the previous two games — just six minutes in. After sitting the entire fourth quarter, he began the overtime fresh, as he scored eight more points and combined with Reggie Miller to score all of Indiana's 14 points in the extra session. Smits finished with 24 points on 11-for-14 shooting.

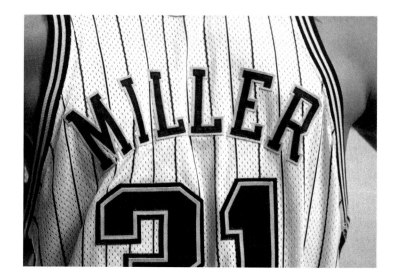

With the hopes of a team, a crowd and a city sitting atop Reggie Miller's shoulders, was there any doubt who would get the last shot as the Pacers inbounded the ball with 5.9 seconds to go. Miller did have an opening on the right wing, with Smits as the option inside for a two-pointer and double-overtime. Going for the tie as an option - not to Miller. It was going to be all or nothing. But as Miller rose to release the ball, the Lakers' Robert Horry was flying out to contend and Miller had to adjust the arc of his shot — but not enough. "It felt good," he said. "I think what more distracted me was when Robert Horry was running at me. I had to shoot it higher over his hand. When you do that, you've probably got to shoot it a little bit longer, which I didn't."

After it finally ended, Phil Jackson and his Lakers stood one victory away from their final destination, from the ultimate award for their blood, toil, tears and sweat. "We know it's going to take another effort like that to close this out on Friday," Jackson said, "if we can possibly get it."

Game 4

LAKERS

PLAYER	POS	MIN	FGM-A	3PM-A	FTM-A	OFF	DEF	TOT	AST	PF	ST	TO	BS	PTS
Rice	F	39	3-8	2-3	3-3	0	1	1	1	3	0	3	0	11
Green	F	16	2-2	0-0	1-2	1	2	3	0	3	0	0	0	5
O'Neal	C	47	13-25	0-0	10-17	7	14	21	1	6	2	3	2	36
Bryant	G	47	14-27	0-0	0-0	2	2	4	5	4	1	3	2	28
Harper	G	26	2-6	0-2	0-0	0	3	3	2	2	0	0	0	4
Fox		15	3-5	1-2	1-1	1	2	3	2	5	0	1	0	8
Horry		37	6-10	0-2	5-7	2	4	6	2	4	2	1	0	17
Fisher		20	3-6	1-2	0-0	0	0	0	4	2	1	1	0	7
Shaw		13	2-4	0-1	0-0	1	0	1	3	0	0	0	0	4
Salley		5	0-0	0-0	0-0	0	0	0	0	2	0	0	0	0
Knight		DNP - Coach's Decision												
George		DNP - Coach's Decision												
TOTAL		265	48-93	4-12	20-30	14	28	42	20	31	6	12	4	120
			(51.6)	(33.3)	(66.7)				Team Rebs: 10		Total TO: 12 (11 Pts)			

PACERS

PLAYER	POS	MIN	FGM-A	3PM-A	FTM-A	OFF	DEF	TOT	AST	PF	ST	TO	BS	PTS
Rose	F	44	5-16	0-0	4-4	0	3	3	5	3	1	3	0	14
Davis	F	29	2-4	0-0	0-2	2	6	8	0	6	1	0	0	4
Smits	C	22	11-14	0-0	2-2	1	2	3	0	4	1	2	2	24
Miller	G	50	9-19	6-9	11-12	0	5	5	3	1	1	1	1	35
Jackson	G	32	2-8	1-3	2-2	0	2	2	7	2	0	1	0	7
Croshere		19	3-6	0-1	4-4	1	6	7	1	3	0	1	0	10
Perkins		22	3-6	3-5	1-2	0	4	4	2	5	0	1	0	10
Best		21	5-9	0-1	0-0	2	0	2	4	2	0	2	0	10
McKey		23	2-2	0-0	0-0	3	2	5	0	2	1	1	0	4
Mullin		3	0-0	0-0	0-0	0	0	0	0	0	0	0	0	0
Tabak		DNP - Coach's Decision												
Bender		DNP - Coach's Decision												
TOTAL		265	42-84	10-19	24-28	9	30	39	22	28	5	12	3	118
			(50.0)	(52.6)	(85.7)				Team Rebs: 10		Total TO: 13 (16 Pts)			

| Game 5 – June 16, 2000 |

Pacers 120   Lakers 87

Somewhere in a secluded recess of Conseco Fieldhouse, not far from the visitors' dressing room, the chilled bottles sat waiting patiently. Their destiny would be to take part in a joyous celebration, a party that would see their contents spraying and soaking everything purple and gold; a coronation and confirmation that the Lakers glory days had returned.

"They're still the team in control, they're still the team with three,
but we're still the team that has fight." Jalen Rose

Well before the final buzzer sounded, the party had already begun – but without those bottles of bubbly. Far be it for the gods of basketball to allow any gala on Indiana hardwood that wasn't in honor of one of their own. For the Pacers, to even conceive of having to watch the Lakers stomp and shake with their new NBA championship on sacred ground was something they would simply not allow. And to have that happen after Larry Bird's final game as Indiana coach? Not in their house.

"We heard about the parade they have planned," said a grinning Jalen Rose, who powered the Pacers with 32 points, including four three-pointers as the Pacers sliced Los Angeles' series lead to 3-2. "That won't be tomorrow, though."

"So many people got ready for a celebration tonight," said Mark Jackson, "which was disrespectful to us and the character that we have on this basketball team."

From the outset, the Pacers' agenda was clear. As the fans filling the Fieldhouse roared in approval, Indiana responded by shooting the lights out; a blistering 15-for-20 in the first

quarter alone, including six-of-six from three-point range. By the time it was over, the Pacers had put up some of the gaudiest numbers any team had against the Lakers this season, as they shot better than 57 percent from the field, won the battle on the glass with conviction and buried 10 three-pointers.

The assault escalated and the benches emptied, and it ended with Los Angeles not only absorbing its worst loss of the year, but rekindling the mutters regarding its repeated difficulty in closing out series, in becoming pacifists when a killer instinct is needed. Even though they could take comfort in the thought of returning to STAPLES Center and accomplishing their mission there, Phil Jackson wasn't especially pleased with what he had witnessed.

"I don't like to think of a team that has championship quality in it that loses by 33 points," the coach said before the flight back home to L.A. "We have to prove something to ourselves when we go back home in that regard."

Three nights later, the Lakers – with those unopened bottles still waiting – would have that opportunity.

With their team on the brink of summer, Reggie Miller and Jalen Rose could not have chosen a better time to combine for 57 points, eight three-pointers, 11-for-11 free-throw shooting, 10 rebounds and 11 assists. They consistently found the openings and cashed in on their countless open looks. Rose was outright stellar — 32 points, including four three-pointers — and drove the lane with abandon, holding nothing back. And Miller stayed right in step with 25. "Anytime both of those guys, Reggie and Jalen, are having big nights at the same time, it makes it almost impossible to guard them," said teammate Austin Croshere, "because you can't double-team either one of them. The other one is going to be open." And they were. Again and again.

"It's important for us not to allow them to celebrate winning the championship, no matter where they do it." **Mark Jackson**

The notion of having the season end before their eyes was something the partisan Conseco Fieldhouse gathering of 18,345 did not even consider. And thanks to the Pacers seconding that emotion, the ride did not end inside Indiana's masterpiece of an arena. "After the last game, I talked about us not allowing [the Lakers] to celebrate on our floor," Miller said. "I was serious about that. That would be a bad feeling to end our season on." But on this night, there would be nothing of the sort for those who bleed Pacers blue and gold.

He has successfully transcended time — from "The Hick From French Lick" to "Larry Legend" to simply "Coach." And in his last game as the coach of the Indiana Pacers at Conseco Fieldhouse, Larry Bird was able to savor the sweetness of victory. He was already the winningest playoff coach in Pacers history, and second on the franchise's all-time coaching list. Fittingly, he deflected attention away from himself when asked about the personal significance of the evening's events. "I think it's very important for us to come out and assure our fans we're not going to quit." Spoken like a true legend.

It was hardly a coincidence that in the Pacers' two Finals victories on their home floor, they were able to surpass the Lakers' efforts under the boards. In Game 5, the discrepancy was a glaring 46-34. The bulk of the effort, as in the series' previous battles, was provided by Croshere, Dale Davis and Sam Perkins, who combined for 24. Croshere, in fact, nearly pulled off a double-double — 13 points and nine rebounds — in 25 minutes off the bench. But that trio was hardly alone in its glass cleaning; Rose and Mark Jackson chipped in with six apiece.

"I'm sure they'll just throw this game away. They probably won't even watch the film. They'll come out aggressive on Monday and go after it." Reggie Miller

During pregame warmups, the Pacers' most potent pair of point-producers huddled for a few moments, and the two agreed the night would be one their fans would not forget. And by the time it was over, they and their teammates reveled in the elation they had helped fuel. "It was the last game for a lot of guys in there," Miller said. "We're facing elimination." Said Rose: "Indiana thrives on basketball. For this to be happening for our town, we didn't want them to leave today's game feeling like the season was a disappointment." Judging by the decibel level inside Conseco Fieldhouse at the final buzzer, it was anything but.

Two nights before, he had put on an exhibition that was nothing less than magnificent, but Kobe Bryant was unable to match himself. Clearly, the weather — not to mention the Pacers' tight defense — had grounded Air Kobe to a pedestrian 4-for-20, eight-point night. But Bryant refused to take his off-night too much to heart, knowing his Lakers still had two chances to get the one victory that would propel them to the Promised Land. "We're a little disappointed," he said with an infectious, unaffected smile. "But it's really no biggie when you think about it."

"I didn't have a good game tonight.
You know, you just bounce back." Kobe Bryant

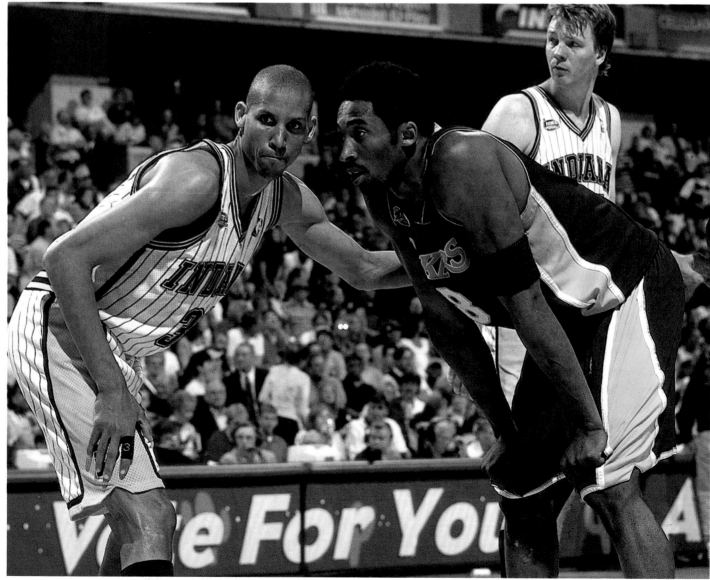

He was seven years removed from his last All-Star appearance and 15 from his first NBA game, but Chris Mullin had become a forgotten man on the deep, forward-heavy Pacers roster —
until there was 4:50 remaining and Mullin relieved Miller to a thunderous ovation. And there were probably almost as many among the Conseco faithful cheering for the popular Mullin as there were
for Miller. The crescendo then caromed off the roof with 1:17 to play, when Mullin drained a 17-footer, and the 36-year-old veteran enjoyed what used to be a common moment in the spotlight.

Game 5

LAKERS PLAYER	POS	MIN	FGM-A	3PM-A	FTM-A	OFF	DEF	TOT	AST	PF	ST	TO	BS	PTS
Rice	F	30	3-8	1-2	4-7	0	0	0	2	2	1	1	0	11
Green	F	16	3-4	0-0	1-1	1	1	2	0	2	0	0	0	7
O'Neal	C	42	17-27	0-0	1-6	7	4	11	3	2	2	3	2	35
Bryant	G	37	4-20	0-1	0-0	1	4	5	3	5	2	0	0	8
Harper	G	25	3-8	2-4	0-0	2	3	5	5	2	1	2	0	8
Fox		15	0-1	0-1	1-1	0	0	0	0	2	1	0	0	1
Horry		29	3-8	1-6	0-0	0	4	4	2	5	0	1	0	7
Fisher		22	0-6	0-3	2-2	1	1	2	1	3	2	1	0	2
Shaw		12	0-4	0-1	0-0	0	1	1	2	4	0	2	0	0
Salley		4	2-2	0-0	0-0	1	2	3	0	2	0	0	0	4
Knight		5	1-1	0-0	1-2	0	0	0	0	2	0	1	0	3
George		3	0-1	0-1	1-2	0	1	1	0	2	0	1	0	1
TOTAL		240	36-90	4-19	11-21	13	21	34	18	33	9	12	2	87
			(40.0)	(21.1)	(52.4)					Team Rebs: 12	Total TO: 12 (19 Pts)			

PACERS PLAYER	POS	MIN	FGM-A	3PM-A	FTM-A	OFF	DEF	TOT	AST	PF	ST	TO	BS	PTS
Rose	F	44	12-18	4-5	4-4	0	6	6	5	4	2	5	1	32
Davis	F	23	4-7	0-0	0-0	1	7	8	1	3	0	0	0	8
Smits	C	14	5-7	0-0	2-2	1	1	2	0	5	0	0	0	12
Miller	G	39	7-12	4-6	7-7	0	4	4	6	1	1	2	1	25
Jackson	G	30	4-9	0-2	2-2	2	4	6	7	0	0	5	0	10
Croshere		25	1-3	0-0	11-12	1	8	9	3	3	1	2	1	13
Perkins		29	2-7	2-6	0-0	1	6	7	1	3	0	0	0	6
Best		10	2-2	0-0	1-2	0	0	0	3	1	0	0	0	5
McKey		12	0-0	0-0	0-0	0	3	3	0	1	1	0	0	0
Mullin		5	1-2	0-1	2-3	0	0	0	0	0	1	0	1	4
Tabak		5	1-1	0-0	0-0	0	0	0	0	3	0	0	0	2
Bender		4	0-0	0-0	3-4	0	1	1	0	0	1	0	0	3
TOTAL		240	39-68	10-20	32-36	6	40	46	26	24	7	14	4	120
			(57.4)	(50.0)	(88.9)					Team Rebs: 5	Total TO: 16 (13 Pts)			

Lakers 116 Pacers 111

"We are going to be home. Our place is going to be rockin', our place is going to be loud, our place is going to be hostile. We'll be ready." Shaquille O'Neal

All season, he had found delight in unusual but creative self-descriptions — The Big Aristotle, The Big Historical, The Big Continuous. For O'Neal, however, one Big Proclamation was missing. When the final buzzer blared through the air inside a delirious STAPLES Center on June 19, however, O'Neal could finally put the dream into words:

THE BIG CHAMPION delivered **THE BIG TITLE!**

O'Neal barely had time to raise his index fingers into the air to officially signify the Lakers' 2000 NBA championship when Kobe Bryant – who was not yet 10 years old when the Lakers won their last title in 1988 – jumped into his arms. The moment was genuine, spontaneous and perfect because O'Neal, the patent officer of monikers, already had coined labels for the twosome — "The Combo," "The One-Two Punch" and "The Hip-Hop Version of Kareem and Magic."

The moment was significant, too, because on the final night of NBA Finals 2000, Shaq and Kobe put on a show worthy of Oscar nomination. Shaq amassed 41 points and seized 12 rebounds while Kobe carved his place in NBA Finals lore with 26 points and 10 rebounds. In the fourth quarter, the two combined for 21 points and seven rebounds to wrest control of the game from the pumped-up Pacers.

The climactic act was really an anticlimax; O'Neal, devastating throughout the series, was named the unanimous MVP of the NBA Finals, and became the eighth player to be named regular-season and Finals MVP in the same season. After averaging 38 points and 16 rebounds in the six-game triumph, it was no surprise. When it was over, O'Neal stood in the middle of the party, on the STAPLES Center floor, surrounded by family, friends and teammates … and cried.

"I held emotion for about 11 years now," he said. "Three years of college, eight years in the league, always wanting to win. This is what I wanted to come to the NBA for. It just came out."

Said teammate Ron Harper: "Whatever he wants to call himself, we rode him to a championship."

The 18,997 who packed STAPLES Center for the clinching game were loud and raucous, a departure from the stereotypical L.A. gatherings that arrive late and leave early, and even spelled out their feelings about the Lakers in the closing moments of the game.

He had almost willed a seventh and deciding game, but Reggie Miller and the Pacers would experience the agony of reaching out for the NBA's ultimate prize, only to have it snatched away. With a chance to tie Game 6 in the final minute, his long three-point attempt from the left wing found nothing but iron. "I tried to get the first look I possibly could," he said. "I probably could have took the ball off the dribble and got an easy layup, but I'm never one to do things easy. I wanted to tie up the ballgame right there."

In Los Angeles, the past, present and future of the Lakers is intertwined, and proof came afterward, when Magic Johnson joined the celebration. Now the a team co-owner/vice president, Johnson knows something about winning, having claimed five championship rings during his career.

"I tell you, that is the best duo that I've seen in a long time. And they are going to be around forever." Glen Rice, on Shaquille O'Neal and Kobe Bryant

The NBA 2000 championship was the sixth for Lakers owner Dr. Jerry Buss. The players had his praise, but Buss reserved special thanks for the fans.

"I'm very proud of the fans. Everybody told us that the best fans are in other cities — that's crazy. The best fans are in L.A."

Phil Jackson was one connection between championship rings in Chicago and Los Angeles. Ron Harper was another. After being fitted for jewelry three times with the Bulls, Harper came to the Lakers and proved a valuable source of veteran leadership. "There's no way to put it into words," Harper said. "Who ever thought in 1986, when I came up, that I'd have four championship rings now? I never dreamed that. There have been a lot of great players in the league that don't have any rings. I can't compare. They're all awesome."

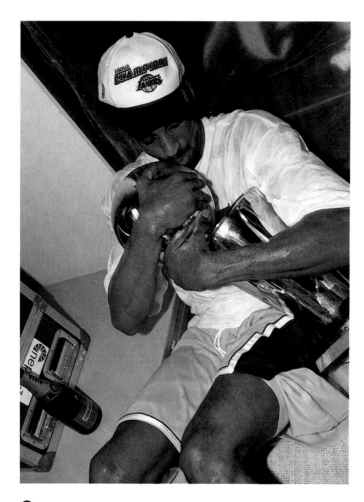

After the party on the floor, after the flow of champagne, after the last sound bite, Shaquille O'Neal was left to ponder the moment with his sparkling new Finals MVP trophy, and all the emotion of an entire career without a championship spilled out. He had actually cried on the court for all to see, but he managed to save more for later. "Tears were coming to my eyes because I've been working hard in my life," he said. "I took a lot of bashing." Said teammate Glen Rice: "He's taken a lot of criticism over the years because he hasn't won the big one. And now he's won it."

It was almost as if he was growing up right before the eyes of the basketball world. Only four years ago, he was in high school and he still seems like such a kid — except, of course, on the court. In Game 6, Kobe Bryant's maturing process seemed to shift into overdrive. With one minute to play in the first half, Indiana led by nine. But a steal by Bryant was the catalyst for six straight points, including his 26-foot three-pointer with only 2.3 ticks before the break. Suddenly, the Pacers' advantage had been sliced to three.

"We're going to get one next year, too."

Shaquille O'Neal

"Are we looking forward to coming back next year
and defending our throne? Absolutely." *Kobe Bryant*

Game 6

PACERS						REBOUNDS								
PLAYER	POS	MIN	FGM-A	3PM-A	FTM-A	OFF	DEF	TOT	AST	PF	ST	TO	BS	PTS
Rose	F	42	9-20	2-3	9-11	1	0	1	3	3	0	2	0	29
Davis	F	35	8-10	0-0	4-6	5	9	14	3	4	0	0	3	20
Smits	C	25	1-8	0-0	0-0	2	4	6	1	5	0	1	1	2
Miller	G	40	8-19	2-10	7-7	0	1	1	3	1	1	2	0	25
Jackson	G	40	3-7	2-4	2-2	0	8	8	11	3	1	1	0	10
Croshere		23	4-7	3-5	5-6	1	4	5	0	5	0	1	1	16
Perkins		13	2-2	2-2	0-0	0	4	4	1	1	0	1	0	6
Best		8	0-2	0-0	0-0	0	1	1	2	1	0	0	0	0
McKey		14	1-2	1-1	0-0	0	1	1	0	4	0	1	1	3
Mullin		DNP - Coach's Decision												
Tabak		DNP - Coach's Decision												
Bender		DNP - Coach's Decision												
TOTAL		240	36-77	12-25	27-32	9	32	41	24	27	2	9	6	111
			(46.8)	(48.0)	(84.4)				Team Rebs: 8		Total TO: 9 (21 Pts)			

LAKERS						REBOUNDS								
PLAYER	POS	MIN	FGM-A	3PM-A	FTM-A	OFF	DEF	TOT	AST	PF	ST	TO	BS	PTS
Rice	F	35	5-7	3-3	3-6	0	6	6	2	3	1	0	0	16
Green	F	20	2-3	0-0	2-2	3	2	5	0	1	1	1	0	6
O'Neal	C	47	19-32	0-0	3-12	5	7	12	1	2	0	0	4	41
Bryant	G	45	8-27	2-6	8-9	3	7	10	4	4	1	1	2	26
Harper	G	37	3-10	0-2	0-0	0	3	3	9	2	2	1	0	6
Fox		14	1-1	1-1	4-4	1	0	1	1	3	0	0	0	7
Horry		27	3-6	2-3	0-0	1	3	4	4	6	0	2	1	8
Fisher		8	2-3	2-2	0-0	0	1	1	3	1	0	0	0	6
Shaw		7	0-1	0-0	0-0	0	2	2	1	2	0	0	0	0
Salley		DNP - Coach's Decision												
Knight		DNP - Coach's Decision												
George		DNP - Coach's Decision												
TOTAL		240	43-90	10-17	20-33	13	31	44	25	24	5	5	7	116
			(47.8)	(58.8)	(60.6)				Team Rebs: 13		Total TO: 5 (8 Pts)